Designed By You:
Ideas and Inspiration for Rug Hookers

By Tamara Pavich

Presented by

RUG HOOKING

Copyright © 2017 by Ampry Publishing LLC

Published by
AMPRY PUBLISHING LLC
3400 Dundee Road, Suite 220
Northbrook, IL 60062
www.amprycp.com

www.rughookingmagazine.com

All rights reserved, including the right to reproduce this book or portions thereof in any form or by any means, electronic or mechanical, including photocopying, recording, or by any information storage and retrieval system, without permission in writing from the publisher. All inquiries should be addressed to *Rug Hooking* Magazine, 3400 Dundee Road, Suite 220, Northbrook, IL 60062

Printed in the United States of America

10 9 8 7 6 5 4 3 2 1

Photography by the artists unless otherwise noted.

Cataloging-in-Publication Data
Library of Congress Control Number: 2017934751

ISBN 9781945550072

Contents

Kopp Wedding Rug, *51" x 30½", #8-cut wool on linen. Designed and hooked by Tamara Pavich, Council Bluffs, Iowa, 2009. The images come from the folk-art book of Joel and Kate Kopp. I used templates to draw it on linen. The circa 1900 image implies the story of a bride, standing on her tiny rug beseeching a moon-faced being in the night sky. Her groom, who may be real or imaginary, alive or dead, appears in a halo of light, and intertwining vines festooned with hearts connect the pair.*

4
Acknowledgments

5
Introduction

6
Chapter 1
Generating Ideas for Designing Your Rugs

26
Chapter 2
Begin Drawing, So That You Can Draw

42
Chapter 3
Start with a Style

58
Chapter 4
Start with Color

74
Chapter 5
Start with Art

94
Chapter 6
Start with Materials

110
Chapter 7
Start with a Story

126
Chapter 8
Start with Yourself

143
Conclusion

144
Recommendations for Further Inspiration

Acknowledgments

When I began writing for *Rug Hooking* magazine a few years ago, I soon learned that there are about three degrees of separation between the hookers on this earth. Wanda Kerr helped me find Val Flannigan, Diane Cox, and Kay LeFevre. Janet Conner helped me find Norma Brimstein and Deb Walland. Deb Smith helped me find Brigitte Webb, way over in Scotland. In turn, Brigitte introduced me to the work of Håkon Grøn Hensvold, a marvelous rug hooker in Norway.

You hold in your hands the product of many imaginations, and I hope you will savor this trove of original designs.

Unlike most authors of rug-hooking books, I am not a teacher. I have taught writing and literature courses, but I don't aspire to teach other people how to hook rugs. I'm not in any kind of rug-hooking business, but writing this book combines three of my passions: a love of the written word, the joy of making rugs, and the hope that this volume will be just the encouragement you need to cut a nice piece of linen, pick up that marker, and draw your first original design.

While writing, I have depended on the expertise of my teachers and fellow rug hookers. For their generosity, I am more grateful than I can say. From some teachers, I have been fortunate to take a class. I have read the books of others. In the case of Janet Conner, we have talked on the phone and emailed profusely, having never met in person. Yet, each of these wise friends is responsible for part of the content here. Some friends have hooked original designs that were needed for this book, a gesture of true friendship if ever there was one.

I am grateful that my family members are present in this volume, either through our stories, their own hookings (Mom, Lori, and Ann), their artworks that I have adapted (David's pencil sketches), or in their likenesses (Isabella, Christian, Grace, and our late Aunt Ann). Thanks also to Pete, the photographer in the family, for taking many of my rug photos, and to Dad for his example and encouragement for nearly 60 years. My husband always listens patiently to my latest project idea and says, "Sure. Go for it." Thank you, Mike.

May we continue to explore and find new acquaintances in the great web of rug hookers, and may we inspire each other to be curious, creative, magnanimous, resourceful, and kind.

Warmest thanks to the following teachers and friends:

Lou Ann Ayres	*Karen Marie Greenfield*	*Holly McMillan*
Terri Bangert	*Denise Hoffman*	*Becky Pearson*
Linda Boehle	*Donna Hrkman*	*Lilly Phillips*
Luci Bolding	*Jodi Isom*	*Jane Scott*
Pris Buttler	*Mary Jo Lahners*	*Cathy Stephan*
Janet Conner	*Anne-Marie Lewis*	*Lori Stopak*
Ann Eastman	*Roslyn Logsdon*	*Anita White*

The late Ann Wiseman
And all the hookers of the rugs in these pages

Special thanks to Karen, Holly, Pris, Janet, Cathy, and Anita.
And to my mom, Lilly, my Tooth Fairy.

Introduction: You Can Draw

If you hear a voice within you say "you cannot paint," then by all means paint and that voice will be silenced.

—Vincent Van Gogh

Throughout my life, I have said these words a hundred times: "Me? I can't draw." I believed that. I believed it until rug hooking changed my mind, with the help of Holly McMillan.

In every group, there is a brave soul who will try anything, and Holly has been that person in our rug-hooking circle. Like all of us, she has certainly hooked her share of commercial patterns—with delightful color-planning—but long before the rest of us, she drew her own designs too, moving quickly from simple drawings to much more complex images of her home state of Nebraska. Holly has adapted family photographs and familiar landscapes. She has restricted color in her monochromatic rugs, and she's gone wild with color to the delight of her children. Gradually, her freedom to draw images that spoke to her became an infectious influence on our rug-hooking group. Looking at the variety and beauty in her rugs, we all wanted to try it. She was among the most enthusiastic participants in our first group challenge and continues to encourage us to greater challenges. Now that we're all getting into the design groove with her, she applauds the patterns that many of us are drawing ourselves.

To draw rug designs, we don't have to possess the talents of Renoir or Van Gogh. For instance, I have discovered that I am capable of drawing the funny-looking, lopsided, amateur, doodle-sketches, which you will soon see. However, once I learned that my simple drawings could result in a perfectly nice rug, I grew bolder, and I have been drawing my own rug patterns for years. Understand, please, that I have not become a better artist—well, maybe a bit better—but drawing at my level doesn't frighten me anymore.

The rug always turns out a little different from the drawing, and that's not necessarily disappointing. Now I know that the magic ingredient, wool, will transform my picture into something else altogether.

Many rug hookers allow their lack of artistic confidence to hold them back. While they could be hooking the images that express their stories, while they could be developing their own style and subject matter and producing a body of original work, they limit themselves instead to hooking only commercial patterns. They thumb through *Rug Hooking* magazine and sigh over the originality on those pages. At workshops and rug shows, they look longingly at the designs of others and continue to repeat my tired refrain: "Me? I can't draw."

This book, however, can take you, step-by-easy-step, idea by idea, toward expressing yourself through original designs. Here, you'll find suggestions for generating ideas—from memory, from nature, from art, and from friendship. If you need help to begin drawing, Chapter 2 will offer a wealth of methods and resources. The majority of these pages provide our readers with about thirty-six concrete ideas to draw, each with hooked examples to stir your imagination. Every section of the book begins with an easy-to-render design idea and ends with a more challenging one.

It is our sincere hope that all of our readers will learn just how forgiving the art of rug hooking is and how a modest drawing will result in a memorable rug. May you be inspired to enter a new phase of self-expression. And before long, may you hold in your hands the first of many rugs *Designed By You*.

1

Generating Ideas for Designing Your Rugs

You Swim, *27" x 14½", #8-cut wool on linen. Designed and hooked by Sharon Townsend, Altoona, Iowa 2013.*

"While taking our tug boat down the Mississippi, down the Ohio, up the Tennessee, and on to the Tenn-Tom waterway headed to Florida," Sharon said, "my husband and I ran into a bit of trouble. We had spent the night tied up to a dock in the middle of nowhere above Demopolis, Alabama. When we went to leave in the morning, the motor would not start. We called a nearby marina, and the mechanic said we had probably picked up a rope. Someone needed to check, he said. Bob looked at me and said, 'You swim.' So here I am in the muddy water under the boat, feeling around for the rope, with Bob safely directing from above.

"I worked on this piece in Evelyn Lawrence's story class at Sauder. She suggested it, as I had told her the story years before."

In our minds, each of us has a trove of meaningful images: an oak leaf, our grandmother's quilt pattern, Dad's Navy photo, a Grant Wood painting, the view from our kitchen window, a dear old watering can. In fact, that's often why a particular commercial rug pattern appeals to us. Often the pattern resonates with an image we have always loved. Whether you know it or not, you have been collecting such images all your life.

But how do we go from someone with a bank of mental images to someone who transforms them into rug designs? The answer is HABITS. You'll find more habits in Chapter 2, but for now, let's begin with these three:

Habit #1: Mine your memory

As a new rug designer, you must take time to filter through your memory bank for images that are significant for you, and, importantly, to record them in your journal or sketchbook (see Chapter 2). You will find more than you can ever hook, and as you record memories and stories, the most important ones will float to the top, begging to be drawn and hooked. Please use this chapter to stimulate your memory.

The Iuka Christmas Card, *20" x 14", #3- and 4-cut wool on linen. Adapted from a linoleum block by Warren Taylor, circa 1960. Designed and hooked by Rayna C. Taylor, San Antonio, Texas, 2015.*

This adaptation preserves a part of the Taylor family history. Rayna's father-in-law made the original linoleum block of the snow-covered house, used to make the family Christmas card. Rayna has hooked more than one version of this image, and this was her second adaptation.

Habit #2: Become an image collector

Your second task as a rug designer is to continually add to your bank of inspiring images. Ideas can come from anywhere. The art of friends and family can inspire a design, like the lino-cut of Rayna Taylor's father-in-law, which captures the family home so beautifully. Tune your attention to rug-design potential and, using the content of this chapter, become a collector of images.

Habit #3: Build your own confidence

If designing is new for you, you must be encouraged and stay encouraged. Nurture and protect your confidence by gauging the appropriate level of difficulty as you grow. You may be someone who loves to stretch and challenge yourself. Or you may need to start designing with simpler ideas, upon which you can build. This chapter, and indeed this entire book, is filled with design ideas to spark your imagination, some simple, others complex and advanced. As you cultivate the habits of art, do yourself the favor of assessing where you are now and selecting design ideas that give you success.

Gold Star, *12" x 12", #4-cut wool and acrylic yarn on linen. Designed and hooked by Trish Johnson, Toronto, Ontario, 2016.*

Trish specifically suggested this rug as an example of an extremely simple way of generating a design idea. In response to her guild's challenge, "Going for Gold," Trish bought a package of little star stickers and stuck them to a sticky note in a pleasing arrangement. Next, she scanned the image into her computer and enlarged it. "These are primary colors," Trish said, "red, blue, and yellow, though the yellow is pushed to gold and the red is lightened to pink." The acrylic yarn hooked into the background has "gold metallic bits," Trish said. It's important to note that Trish's rugs have been featured in Celebration *no less than nine times, yet she still loves to use simple designs to explore shapes and color.*

The Simplicity of Shapes

Build a file of geometric shapes from drawings you have created by hand. This gives you a collection of ideas to play with when you are designing.

—Rick Hedof, illustrator

This summer, I found myself too busy to commit to a complicated rug-hooking project. I needed something easy and pretty to get my mind off of work. So I thought about color and the simplest way I could play with it--using circles, all kinds of circle designs. I began with a sundial pillow. Next, a yin-yang chair seat. Then a moon and stars design. In my sketchbook, I drew more circle-play designs than I could hook. Linda Smith has her own ways of designing around the shape of a circle, resulting in rugs that evoke cabbages, a salad bowl, and a primitive flower garden.

Sit down and draw shapes: geometric shapes, like triangles and diamonds; coloring-book shapes, like houses, leaves, or padulas; or abstract shapes like an amoeba or the pieces of a jigsaw puzzle. Arrange your shapes in an appealing way, and then commit them to linen and hook. Some of the most accomplished hookers will tell you that they got started designing by playing with shapes. You can, too.

LEFT: Sundial Pillow, *15" round, #8- and 8.5-cut wool on linen. Designed and hooked by Tamara Pavich, Council Bluffs, Iowa, 2015.* PETER C. PHILLIPS
Keeping design simple allows us to experiment with color combinations.

RIGHT: Yin-Yang Chair Seat, *14" round, #7- and 8-cut wool on linen. Designed and hooked by Tamara Pavich, Council Bluffs, Iowa, 2015.* PETER C. PHILLIPS
The yin-yang symbol is another way of using the simple circle to inspire a design.

Winter Cabbages, *26" x 16", hand-cut recycled wool sweaters and #7-cut wool on linen. Designed and hooked by Linda Smith, Kingston, Ontario, 2013.*

We include three rugs from Linda Smith, each of which uses the humble circle for its basis of design. "This is a maquette for a larger monochromatic wool floor rug that is somewhere in my future," Linda said. "The inspiration comes from the inside vertical cut of a Napa cabbage. Irregular circles hooked in a circular direction."

Roquette, *18" x 20", hand-cut recycled wool, silk, and bamboo fiber on linen. Designed and hooked by Linda Smith, Kingston, Ontario, 2015.*

"Roquette is French for arugula," Linda said. "Some of the vegetables in this salad are circles, like the radishes and beets. Some of the greens have a very circular motion to them. I hooked the background in a circular motion, like a plate."

Blue Posies, *30" x 20", #7-cut and hand-cut recycled wool, sari silk, and wool yarn on linen. Designed and hooked by Linda Smith, Kingston, Ontario, 2015.*

"I used the basic circle to create the blue flowers and smaller white circles to add contrast," Linda said. "The little white circles could be pollen or seed pods that have been caught in the breeze. They add movement to the piece. The flower stems are hooked in sari silk. The gold background is hooked in vertical lines on a hit-or-miss basis. This is a cheery little rug. I was going to put it by the back door, but I can't bring myself to put it on the floor."

Generating Ideas for Designing Your Rugs

Beauty in Humble Things

"... *Bright copper kettles and warm woolen mittens,*
Brown paper packages tied up with string,
These are a few of my favorite things."

—Oscar Hammerstein, My Favorite Things

Fairly recently, the cultural powers-that-be have come to recognize "found objects" as art. One article described a Chicago exhibition that featured a single black glove, found on the street, mounted on the wall and lit as a piece of art. "I've been finding single black gloves, usually two or three a week," noted Jack Earhart, the artist. "I think a lot of people are walking around with one cold hand."

Whether we have some sentimental attachment to an object, or whether we see its shape as artistically interesting, or whether, like Jack Earhart, we infer a story behind the object—the unwitting loss of a glove on an icy sidewalk—humble objects can be the subjects of striking rugs.

Consider the meaning in humble objects, their function as symbols. A symbol, quite simply, is a tangible thing that represents an intangible. The image of a spent candle may represent the passing of time. A pair of muddy work boots may symbolize humility or the value of earnest labor. A book, wisdom. A bicycle, childhood adventure. And so on.

What humble things appeal to you? Look at your surroundings and find something to draw. Designing around one humble thing may be the best way to begin your rug-designing career.

Coffee, *23" x 18", #6- and 8-cut wool on linen. Designed and hooked by Becky Pearson, Genoa, Nebraska, 2015.*

"Co-owning a gourmet espresso shop and managing another shop led me to hook this rug," Becky said. "I serve an eclectic range of people in the shop. Some want theirs in a to-go cup, so I hooked one. Others come in to meet with friends or to study or just to visit with the barista—me!—so the mug and saucer represent them. The coffee beans added whimsy, and so did the beaded inner border and steam extending into the border. I have steamed a lot of milk. Coffee is never boring, no matter how you take it."

Ming Check, *5' x 5', #8- and 4-cut wool on Scottish burlap. Designed and hooked by Nancy Peterson, Glenwood, Iowa, 2011.*

"This rug was inspired by a vintage Chinese Checkers board I picked up at a garage sale," Nancy said. "I love the bold graphics of the old game boards. I knew I wanted to make a room-sized rug without piecing the backing so I found a vendor in Canada who was able to supply me with six-foot-wide burlap for backing. I dyed all the wool, matching the colors in the original gameboard. This is the largest rug I have hooked. I tend to like doing bigger rugs that I can throw on the floor. It took me nine months."

Generating Ideas for Designing Your Rugs 11

The Natural World

Audubon Sand Hill Crane, *21" x 30"(without frame), #3- and 4-cut wool on linen. Adapted from an Audubon postcard illustration. Designed and hooked by Jane Scott, Plattsmouth, Nebraska, 2016.*

"My husband and I went to view the crane migration two years ago," Jane said. "It was amazing! I decided to hook the crane for my granddaughter, who is pursuing a master's degree in applied ecology. We call her 'Sarah Bird.' I began the rug with Victoria Engalls." Jane intentionally hooked the rug on bleached linen with the intention of leaving the background unhooked. Her finished rug in its frame is 25" x 35".

You can put yourself in the way of beauty.

—Cheryl Strayed

Rug designers see rugs everywhere, in every scenic view and in each small blossom. Soon you will have more design ideas than you can possibly execute, simply by turning your attention to the beauty in nature all around you. You may begin by noticing the broader vista, then narrow to close-ups of timid deer, reckless squirrels, or tipsy butterflies. For another shift in perspective, zoom in for close studies of leaves, grasses, and stones.

To gain inspiration from nature, walk regularly in a familiar natural landscape. For me, it's the nature trail along the levee, where I walk winter, spring, summer, and fall, observing the changing landscape as seasons come and go. In summer, the cottonwood trees whisper as I walk by, but by November, they are silent and bare. Even in winter, there is color in the fields.

As you walk, frame up pictures in your imagination. You can stay true to nature's composition and palette, or use what you want and let your imagination have its way. Collect tokens (bird nests, leaves, shells) from nature and bring them home to draw. Keep a sketchpad in your car or carry a digital camera to help you remember your ideas.

Travel can inspire, as our two examples will show. More than a few of my nature rugs have been inspired right here at my kitchen table, as I watch the visitors to my bird feeders: a pair of cardinals, the agile nuthatches, and when we're lucky, the rose-breasted grosbeak. Since we put the suet out, a woodpecker rug seems likely.

Cinque Terre Perspective, *9" x 17", #4-cut wool on linen. Designed and hooked by Val Flannigan, Kelowna, British Columbia, 2014.*

"The idea for this piece started with a class," Val said. "It was Pam Bartlett's Wind and Waves class. I was then on a trip to the Cinque Terre area in Italy with the most spectacular scenery! I took lots and lots of photos. My challenge was to hook realistic rocks and water to get depth and splashes. I chose this photo for those elements. I found that the rocks were the most challenging. I used light, medium, and dark, to get the perspective, and then had to use high contrast to get the depth between the rocks. I dyed a lot of shades of blues in order to get the effect of shallow and deeper water."

Art of All Kinds

Modify or adapt, and you will come up with some individual interpretation of the original that you will have every right to regard as your own.

—Stella Hay Rex

Happiness, 18½" x 18½", #6-, 7-, and 8-cut wool on linen. Adapted with permission from the collage by Elizabeth St. Hilaire Nelson. Designed and hooked by Tamara Pavich, Council Bluffs, Iowa, 2013.

When I first saw the songbird collages of Elizabeth St. Hilaire Nelson, they took my breath away. Rendered in her dazzling signature palette, her images had me gasping and sighing and paging through them again and again. I had to try to hook those pretty birds. Fortunately, Elizabeth gave me permission to adapt several collages. I began with this bluebird in a workshop with teacher and friend, Anita White.

The art world is vast, and no matter how long you explore it, there will always be more to discover. One way to gain artistic confidence is to follow in an artist's footsteps by adapting his/her work. Fledgling artists have imitated the masters for centuries, and many contemporary artists are honored to be asked permission to adapt their works. You need not explicitly adapt a work of art, but rather you may simply take inspiration from it when designing your own rug.

Cultivate the habit of studying art of all kinds:
- Look to ancient arts and designs, like Celtic and Egyptian symbols, Asian art principles, and even Polynesian petroglyphs.
- Stop by a used bookstore and browse the fine-art section, gleaning ideas from master impressionists like Monet, Picasso, Rousseau, and Van Gogh.
- Visit museums or search the internet to study contemporary arts like collage, stained glass, painting, photography, sculpture, and other media.
- Study textile arts for inspiration, such as paisley, tapestry, batik, crewel embroidery, quilting, weaving, and needlework of all kinds.
- And by all means, let the delight of the folk arts continue to provide rug-hooking inspiration.

NOTE: *See our advice about copyright and adaptation on page 78.*

Vestal Virgin, *22" x 55", #4-, 6-, and 8-cut wool on linen. Designed and hooked by Pris Buttler, Gainesville, Georgia, 2013.*

"I have taught classes on hooking in the style of Gustav Klimt," Pris said. "I hooked this one to show that we can capture the essence of Klimt without making a direct copy of his work."

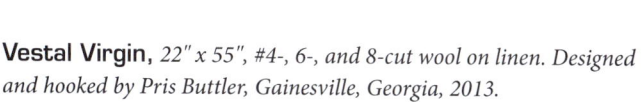

Generating Ideas for Designing Your Rugs

A Stray Word or Phrase

"Words are like eggs dropped from great heights..."
—Jodi Picoult

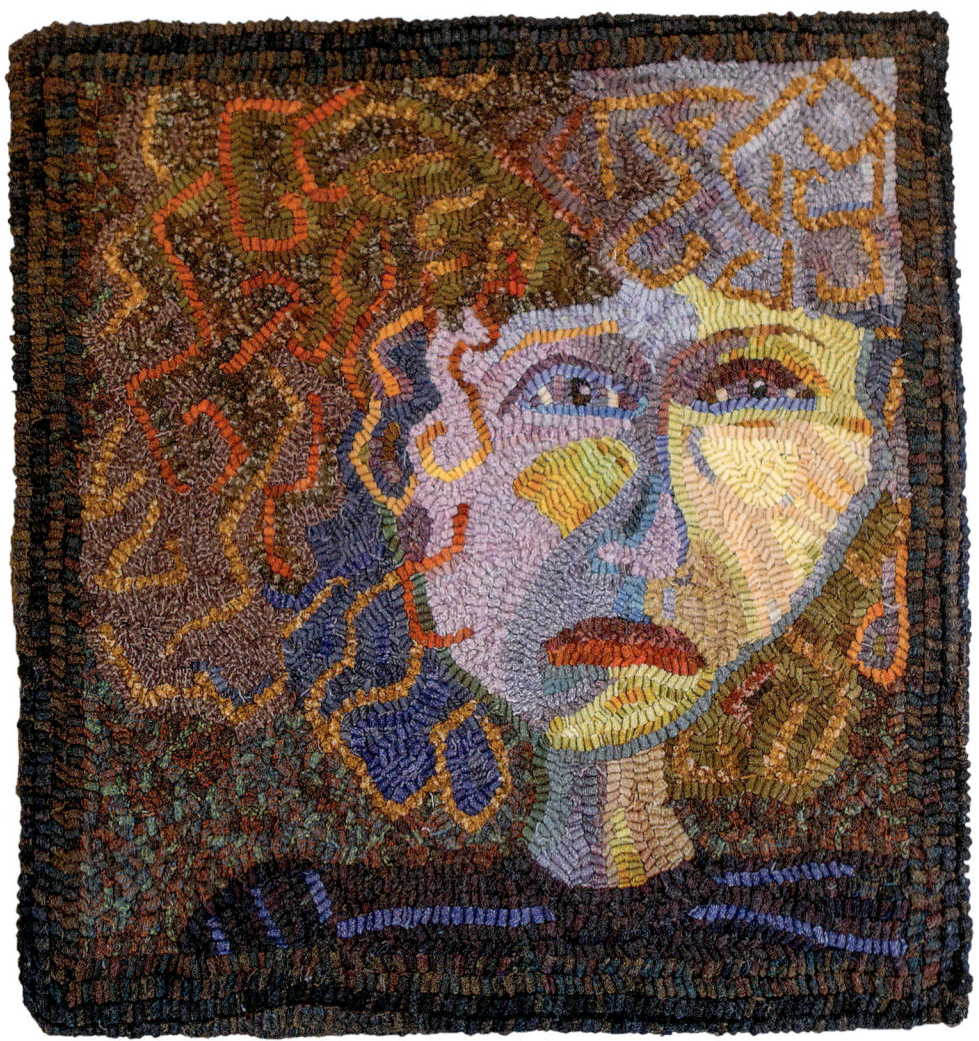

Sometimes a salient turn of phrase is the very thing to inspire a rug design. Words, those black squiggles on a white page, can evoke images in our minds that linger, ferment, and ask to be translated into art. As a collector of images, please don't neglect the written and spoken word as sources to spark your imagination.

Imagine that you're a waiter in a restaurant, gliding around with your tray, gleaning bits of conversation from this table and that one. "Look at these prices!" whispers someone at one table. "Two more dirty martinis, extra olives!" says someone at another table. "He must be running late," says a lone diner. "No gluten. No dairy. No soy," says someone who has just been seated. Notice the scene, the mood, the facial expressions each utterance evokes in your mind. These mini-scenes are born out of words on a page.

Here, you'll find that a descriptive phrase from a magazine article and a misunderstood Bible verse became catalysts for interesting rug designs. Look to advertising slogans or creeds, classic song lyrics, witty tidbits from conversation, and just about any pithy sentence or prose fragment that ignites something within you. Exercise your creative muscles by tuning your ear to a new design idea. It may come from anywhere. Listen closely, or you might miss it.

PREVIOUS PAGE: Imaginary Friend #4, *18" x 18", #6- and 8-cut wool on linen. Designed and hooked by Tamara Pavich, Council Bluffs, Iowa, 2014.* PETER C. PHILLIPS

This rug idea came from a phrase in a magazine article, "hair like yellow pipe cleaners." With the Imaginary Friend series, I was experimenting with facial expression, making this unfortunate friend permanently disappointed. I chose a complementary color scheme, primarily purple and yellow. Her strands of hair are bent into odd angles and shapes.

A Carrot For You, *19½" x 24", #8-cut of wool on linen. Designed and hooked by Sharon Townsend, Altoona, Iowa, 2014.*

Sharon tells a delightful story of a Sunday school lesson, whose message was "He careth for you." As a child, however, she heard "a carrot for you" instead. This design shows her childlike idea of God with his abundance of carrots, like manna from heaven.

Generating Ideas for Designing Your Rugs **17**

The Wool Itself

Flannels, homespun, hard-twist worsted, tweed, jersey, even serge, all work together to give beauty and character to the rug's surface.

—Stella Hay Rex

My friends and I collect textured wools, and from time to time we toss a fat quarter onto the table and ask, "What could we hook with that?"

Whole rugs can be inspired by a little piece of wool that suggests its own subject. What's in your stash? A collection of textures and plaids, wool from recycled clothing, or bright over-dyed flannel? Yarns and other fibers? Visit your shelves, open your totes, caress a skein of yarn and ask yourself, what design could this become? A light-colored tweed may cry out to be Mom's coat, inspiring a small portrait. A small piece of houndstooth may offer the texture in tree bark. A beautiful paisley remnant may bring to mind the plumage of a cardinal. Fluffy yarn may conjure cumulus clouds.

PREVIOUS PAGE: Imaginary Friend #5, *18" x 18", #6- and 7-cut wool and wool yarn on linen. Designed and hooked by Tamara Pavich, Council Bluffs, Iowa, 2015.* PETER C. PHILLIPS

Nola Heidbreder dyed honeycomb wool in three amazing colors--teal, pink, and chartreuse. Those three wools were all the inspiration I needed to draw a new Imaginary Friend with striped hair.

Imaginary Friend #3, *18" x 18", #6- and 7-cut wool, sari silk, dyed seam binding, and various yarns on linen. Designed and hooked by Tamara Pavich, Council Bluffs, Iowa, 2014.* PETER C. PHILLIPS

I had collected many fibers, silks, and wool yarns that I'd never dared to use. My Imaginary Friend series became the place to play with those fibers. I would labor over the faces, and then reward myself with all those fun fibers in the hair. This friend has bright sari silks, dyed seam binding, and two pretty yarns hooked into her mane!

Generating Ideas for Designing Your Rugs 19

Friends Who Inspire

Friends . . . they cherish one another's hopes.
They are kind to one another's dreams.
—Henry David Thoreau

Across the Atlantic Ocean in Cornwall, England, there is a group of rug hookers who like a challenge. Not just any kind of challenge, but a mind-opening group challenge that asks each of them to engage her imagination and design something that is uniquely her own. For one group challenge, Diane Louise Cox went the extra mile, so to speak, taking long walks and collecting odd bits of this and that—broken pottery, marbles, old buttons, doll parts, lost jewelry, and much more. She put a few found treasures into paper bags, one for each group member. The rug hookers blindly chose their bags and opened them, examining the objects inside and allowing their imaginations to make the leap to a rug design. Diane's design appears here.

In Mary Jo Lahners's case, her friend Willie was the subject of a rug design. The two dear friends often took the same classes, and Mary Jo thought it would be nice to have her subject sitting right next to her. Willie's patriotism inspired Mary Jo to use the American flag as her background.

Although I like to scribble in my journal and generate design ideas, I find that I am never as imaginative as when I'm bouncing ideas off of an artistically-minded friend. Nourish each other, share ideas, dare to try, and celebrate the results of your collaborations.

PREVIOUS PAGE: Contemplation, *23" x 23", hand-cut recycled fabrics, cottons, acrylics, and wool, on hessian backing. Designed and hooked by Diane Cox, Penzance, Cornwall, 2013.*

Diane used embroidery on a piece of a Victorian silk quilt, hand-sewn on top of the hooking. "This rug came out of a group challenge," Diane said. "I collect things--broken pottery pieces with writing and beautiful designs, tiny pot lids, glass stoppers and marbles, old buttons, parts of delicate ornaments--that I find in the fields where I walk my dogs. All very inspiring!" Diane put these items into grab bags to be chosen by members of her group. "My bag contained several pieces of an old clay pipe," Diane said, "which immediately brought to mind a picture of an old Romany woman reflecting on her life whilst enjoying her pipe. My drawing was very simple, and as I was hooking her, I felt my way into her personality. She gradually emerged, and the piece of old Victorian silk quilt was perfect for her shawl."

My Friend Willie, *19½" x 21", #5- to 8.5-cut wool on linen. Drawn on linen by Lou Ann Ayres and hooked by Mary Jo Lahners, Lincoln, Nebraska, 2014.* DAVID DALE

Mary Jo had possessed a photo of her good friend Willie for some time, and a workshop with Donna Hrkman gave her the chance to adapt it to a rug. If she looked up from the photo, she had Willie herself, also a rug hooker, sitting right next to her for reference. Mary Jo names Donna Hrkman as a teacher who has shaped her artistic vision and credits her teacher for several aspects of this finished piece. "Donna always knows where to put the shadows and colors," Mary Jo said. It was Mary Jo's idea to place a flag behind Willie, because Willie is very patriotic. But it was at Donna's suggestion that she darken the flag where Willie's shadow would fall. "I wouldn't have thought of that," Mary Jo said. This rug won recognition as an original design in Celebration 2015.

Generating Ideas for Designing Your Rugs 21

Family and Story

What the next generation will value most is not what we owned, but the evidence of who we were and the tales of how we lived.

—Ellen Goodman

We carry many kinds of stories: the ones that have been told in our families for generations, the ones from our own childhoods, and more recent stories of personal milestones or accomplishment.

The ideal way to generate family-story rug designs might be to gather members of your family around a photo album or a slide projector and talk to one another about what you remember. It's always interesting to see what each individual remembers and how our memories differ. Each of us has a slightly different version of the story.

In the chapter Start with a Story, we suggest ways to reduce a story to a single image, your rug design. Some of us may be fortunate to have family photos that can be adapted explicitly, while others may need to construct a composite image that collects images from photos, memory, and sometimes from imagination. Whatever means we use to design our rugs about our family's history, we can be sure that they will be treasured by those who share our memories.

PREVIOUS PAGE: Kathryn Rose, *18" x 19", #2- to 8-cut wool on linen. Adapted from a family photograph. Designed and hooked by Laura Schram, Lincoln, Nebraska, 2010.*

"I have always loved this photo of my mother at a function in the 1950s," Laura said. "Sharon Townsend was teaching a class, and since she specializes in people and faces, I designed this rug for the workshop. My mother looked so glamorous in this chiffon dress, kind of like Jackie O. She managed a women's clothing store during my growing-up years, so her chiffon dress was part of who my mother was. The cigarette and the dress were the fashion of her time. The photo included a lamp and a window behind my mother. I loved the lamp, but I remembered Henri Matisse, one of my favorite artists. In his paintings, many times the subjects were beautiful women in rooms with wallpaper. So my background was inspired by his work.

"I enlarged the photo and then outlined it. I used red-dot tracing fabric to put this design on linen. My friends and I had some special moments while I worked on this rug. My mother passed away in 1996. I felt a reconnection to her every time I picked up the rug and hooked."

Gommy, *18" x 24", #3-, 4-, 6-, and 8-cut wool on linen. Adapted from a family photo, designed, and hooked by Luci Bolding, Omaha, Nebraska, 2015.*

"The photo was taken one year before my grandmother died," Luci said, "the same year that my second son was born. I made this rug for myself because I loved Gommy so much. But when my mom saw the rug, I just had to give it to her. It was intentional that I hooked only part of the background. I felt that I had suggested the background, but I like this piece with the linen showing, and I framed it that way."

Generating Ideas for Designing Your Rugs 23

Personal Mythology

You are the hero of your own story.
—Joseph Campbell

Still Life, *55" x 31" #6-, 8-, and 8.5-cut wool, as well as wool and acrylic yarns, on linen. Designed and hooked by Sharon Townsend, Altoona, Iowa, 2014.*

"The title, Still Life, means 'There's still life in the old girl yet,'" Sharon said. "A green, nude woman with life bursting and flowing out of her seemed to me the right way to picture charging on after the death of my dear husband. I purchased the perfect green wool when Diane Stoffel and I were teaching together at Sebring. I started this piece in her class in Nebraska City, and it has the Diane Stoffel touch. She tweaked the lips. It was great fun adding all the yarn and fabric colors to the amoeba shapes. The irregular border signifies the ups and downs of life."

If you're reading this book, then you are inclined to hook rugs and express yourself through their design. It's also likely that you wish to find and express meaning in your life. People do this differently in different cultures, and a rug hooker may explore an endless variety of paths to making images that are meaningful to her.

We can begin with the values and beliefs we wish to depict in our rugs. Perhaps hard work plays a role in your life story. Yours may be a narrative of caring for others. Maybe faith or love of country has defined your path.

We might think about our heroes and their qualities, or we can invent a heroine out of thin air, someone we admire or who seems to embody our most strongly held ideals. Imagine what your heroine would look like.

Our final chapter, Start with Yourself, will suggest several ways of letting our rugs express ourselves, our beliefs, our day-to-day lives, and who we are.

No Idle Hands, *27" x 44", #7- to 8.5-cut wool on linen. Adapted from a Danish folk illustration. Designed by Cathy Stephan and Karen Marie Greenfield. Hooked by Karen Marie Greenfield, Elk Horn, Nebraska, 2015.* PETER C. PHILLIPS

"I was inspired by my Danish heritage," Karen said. "I grew up in Aalborg, Denmark. The girl is wearing the folk costume from my region. The women of her era were fantastic weavers, spinners, and knitters, and they used plants for dying wool, cotton, and flax. In her costume, I tried to capture the deep, rich, warm colors that I remember so well, and also the light, bright, lush colors of the Danish landscape. This girl had no idle hands. She is walking home wearing her wooden clogs, carrying a wooden milk bucket on her head, which is protected by a cotton pillow. She is also knitting a new pair of socks."

2

Begin Drawing, So That You Can Draw

*I am always doing that which I cannot do,
in order that I may learn how to do it.*

—Pablo Picasso

In recent years, the research of Malcolm Gladwell has shown up everywhere, promising that 10,000 hours of practice can turn any novice into a master. Musicians, craftsmen, writers: anyone who puts in the practice can become proficient in her art within six to ten years' time.

However, for our particular art, there's even better news and greater promise. Rug hookers who want to draw already have many tools at hand to help them put an image on linen. And given the magic ingredient of wool (Wool works wonders!), drawing at the master level is not necessary at all.

You need two qualities in order to begin drawing your own patterns: desire and forgiveness. Do you have the desire to design your own rugs by practicing and by learning a little about drawing, and can you forgive yourself for the amateurish, lop-sided, funny-looking drawings you will make at first?

If so, you are a perfect candidate for learning to draw your own patterns.

The Habit of Sketching

Eventually, you'll buy a few books on drawing, or you'll take a class. You'll discover online drawing tutorials (delightful to watch!) to see how it's done by experts. There is a wealth of resources available to rug hookers who want technical knowledge on how to draw. But for now, the important thing is to make a habit of sketching out your ideas.

Regardless of how well or how poorly you think you do it, start drawing today. I like to buy a 24-pack of colorful markers, then pick up a few cheap thick spiral notebooks and fill them with my rug hooking ideas. You may like colored pencils or crayons. You could buy an actual sketchbook from an art store. Whatever your preferred implements, it's important to start drawing right away.

What kind of drawings interest you? As you begin, you may not even be able to answer that question, so begin with experience. Take a walk outdoors, come home, and fill a few pages with your drawings of simplified trees, tree bark, leaves, fields and hills, butterflies and clouds, houses, mailboxes, barns. If you don't want to begin with elements from the real world, just doodle away, arranging geometric shapes, Celtic knots, interesting squiggles and contours. Sit down in front of a print or a painting on your wall and try to replicate it in your sketchbook. Choose a favorite memory and attempt to draw it on your page. Make several versions of it, honing in on the essence of what you'd like to capture. In fact, make several versions of everything you draw. Most of us don't get it right the first time. We need to experiment and be patient, inching closer to our vision, sketch by sketch.

Wool Works Wonders (WWW)

You are what you repeatedly do.

—Aristotle

Corn Dreams, 27" x 23", torn strips on linen. Designed and hooked by Tamara Pavich, Council Bluffs, Iowa, 2009.
PETER C. PHILLIPS

When you start rug hooking, you want to try everything. I wanted to try a rug using torn strips. My day job involves bicycle touring in Iowa mostly, but also in Nebraska, Missouri, and Oklahoma. So my favorite subject, a fat, pink pig, is pictured in this design, all tuckered out, lying flat on his belly, snoozing beside a cornfield, his bike at a distance.

Remember this sentence: Wool Works Wonders. It's your new mantra.

When we see a glorious finished rug, beautifully composed, color-planned, and executed, it is natural to assume that it resulted from the masterful detailed drawing of a true artist whose abilities are beyond our own. Often, however, this is not the case. The magic of wool can make the simplest of drawings into an exceptional finished product.

Consider the commercial patterns you have hooked. Would we all agree that they are not the most extraordinary works of art we've ever seen? They are simple by design. Yet astonishing transformations occur with the addition of our loops of wool. The same will happen with your unremarkable drawing on linen. Trust yourself, and trust your wool. Whenever you begin to doubt that your own designs can turn out beautifully, remind yourself of your mantra—WWW—Wool Works Wonders.

My Courage-to-Draw Story: Drawing in Phases

I used to draw pigs, because they were round and cute and pink and fat. During my Pig Phase, I probably drew and hooked half a dozen pig rugs, mostly of my own design. Other rugs intervened, but I was on a pig mission.

Then, for a long time, I hooked crows. Something about that common bird attracted me, so I kept drawing their blue-black wings and hooking them, usually shading their feathers with reds and teals. My pig and crow phases aren't over, but I have moved on to other things.

About a year ago, I entered my Face Phase. I availed myself of many wonderful resources: books on hooking portraits by Anne Marie Littenberg and April DeConick and workshops with Donna Hrkman and Cathy Stephan. Still, I needed more practice in between other rugs.

So I sat down with my colorful markers and a fat spiral notebook and began to draw my simple, pedestrian faces. At the beginning of the session, I allowed myself to gaze at one example portrait of a woman's face. Naturally, my first effort looked vaguely like this portrait. From there, I started changing her eye shape, her lips, her age, her posture, her position on the page. I accepted the cartoon nature of my simple drawings and kept filling my notebook. I straightened hair, curled and braided it, heaped it on top of heads, chopped it off. I added pearls, chandelier earrings, a choker necklace, turning the pages and beginning again. New page, new face, new woman. Noses were my biggest challenge, but I kept trying until I could draw a somewhat realistic nose. Soon I found that I was attributing personalities to my little drawings, making them confident, candid, bold, understanding, unhappy, insecure, secretive, disappointed, bashful.

I sketched 22 faces in my book before I decided to draw one on linen. Because I had a lot of cut wool in #6, 7, and 8, I wanted the faces to be the appropriate size—pretty large. I also wanted these rugs to be low-stakes experiments, so I made them 18 inches square to conserve on linen and wool. From my little sketchbook, I selected two drawings to hook, and I drew them freehand on the linen.

To make this practice exercise fun, I brought out all my fun fibers to play with: sari silks and my collection of beautiful yarns that I had hardly touched during my rug-hooking career. Once the difficult work of the facial features was complete, I rewarded myself by hooking heads of hair in a riot of color and fiber.

My resulting rugs, which I made into pillows, are not remarkable. I ended up with several semi-realistic, fairly cartoonish faces. But I enjoy these colorful characters, and I learned a lot about proportion of features and rendering facial expression. I include a couple of these rugs here, along with the modest drawings that preceded them, not because they are exceptional, but just to show what the magic element of wool can do.

Imaginary Friend #1, *18" x 18", #6- to 8-cut wool, wool yarn, dyed seam binding, and sari silk on linen. Designed and hooked by Tamara Pavich, Council Bluffs, Iowa, 2014. While I was driving in rural Minnesota, a red-haired woman drove up out of a ditch on her riding lawn mower. She looked like a truth-teller. I could hardly wait to go home and draw her skeptical expression. She became my first Imaginary Friend.* PETER C. PHILLIPS

Imaginary Friend #2, *18" x 18", #6- to 8-cut wool, wool yarn, dyed seam binding, and sari silk on linen. Designed and hooked by Tamara Pavich, Council Bluffs, Iowa, 2014. These first two Imaginary Friends are confident women. The first seems to be saying "Give me a break," but the second friend seems more friendly and open. I obsessively hooked both of these in just a couple of days while secluded in our family cabin on a lake.*
PETER C. PHILLIPS

Begin Drawing, So That You Can Draw

I had never hooked a series before, but I call this group of funny faces my Imaginary Friends Series. Some are pillows propped here and there. Others are hung on the wall. From time to time, I cut a piece of linen to 18-inches square, choose a cartoonish drawing from my sketchbook, and invent a new personality. In doing so, I add another character to my circle.

My Courage-to-Draw story has a lot to do with following inclinations and drawing in phases. I hope some of you will choose a favorite subject and begin a drawing phase of your own. By recognizing and drawing what attracts you, and by drawing variations that continue to challenge you, you'll gain valuable practice and expertise.

(For more on this subject, see our section on hooking series in Chapter 8.)

Laura's Courage-to-Draw Story: Keep It Simple

Today, Laura Kenney is an accomplished Nova Scotia rug-hooking artist, whose work is hung in galleries and whom bloggers write about. Her recent show, "Surfing the Ironing Board," showcased her well-known character, Judy, who figures in many of her original rug designs. But Laura remembers a time when she had to find the courage to draw, and she volunteered this story of how she gradually developed her own artistic confidence:

"When I started rug hooking," Laura said, "I didn't buy patterns, and my drawing skills weren't the best. So I would keep it simple. Dresses were simple, and so I hooked a series of dresses. Looking back on it, I guess I was playing with color combinations and directional hooking."

"When I started to feel a bit braver, I added arms and legs to the dresses. I did a series of these truncated figures in various ballerina poses. I remember a gallery owner asking me, "Why no heads, Laura?" I wish I could have given her some art-speak response, but the truth was that I just didn't think I could draw heads, so I left them off."

Brown Dress, *15" x 34", #8-cut wool, yarn, sari ribbon, on burlap. Designed and hooked by Laura Kenney, Truro, Nova Scotia, 2009.*

On Break, *15" x 34", #8-cut wool, yarn, sari ribbon, on burlap. Designed and hooked by Laura Kenney, Truro, Nova Scotia, 2009.*

"I did finally add heads, but to this day I keep the faces blank, not because I can't do faces, but just because I like the look.

"If you are intimidated by drawing," Laura said, "I understand. It still makes me nervous, but start simple and remember, the burlap has two sides. If you mess up, flip it over and start again."

Chaos, *13" x 35", #8-cut wool, yarn, sari ribbon, on burlap. Designed and hooked by Laura Kenney, Truro, Nova Scotia, 2009.*

Norma's Courage-to-Draw Story: Make It Yours

The idea of adapting a fine art painting may seem especially intimidating, which is precisely why I invited the indefatigable Norma Brimstein to share her Courage-to-Draw story. Courage to draw is nothing new to Norma.

"I can say that I've never hooked someone else's pattern," Norma said. "I figure that with all the time and effort involved in this hooking business, I want to be able to claim that each rug is completely mine. I don't find it that difficult. Drawing skills really aren't necessary. There are plenty of free images out there to incorporate into your own design. It's really just a matter of rearranging them for your own purposes.

"With the first Van Gogh, I remember that my first step was deciding exactly how much of the painting I wanted to hook. I eliminated almost half of it, everything right of the large tree. Then I took the portion of the print that I had decided to use to Staples and had them enlarge it in black and white.

"Next, I traced the main features—the couple, the two big trees, a few other sketchy tree shapes, the horizon line, the slanted line that defines where the tree bottoms fall—onto my linen backing just to get their placement correct. There was no point in trying to draw all the trees or any of the grass and flowers. I'd go crazy trying to do that.

"First, I hooked the couple, then the large tree on the right, then the tree to the immediate left of the man, and then some of the dark background. From then on, it was just a matter of looking at the original and starting to go back and forth between it and my linen, pretty much working from right to left across the picture. I worked as Van Gogh must have, filling my canvas with color."

Norma's sketch: Norma shared her sketch with us to demonstrate just how little needed to be drawn on the linen initially. Drawing skill was far less important than selecting color and giving close attention to the Van Gogh painting Norma was adapting.

Emily & James's Wedding Rug, 29" x 21", #3- to 8-cut wool (much of it hand-cut) on linen. Adapted from the Van Gogh painting Couple Walking in the Forest (1890). Designed and hooked by Norma Brimstein, Rochester, New York, 2014.

"When I saw this work with its fantastic purple trees, I fell in love with it. This project taught me more about hooking than anything else I'd ever done. Each new color had to be chosen in the moment. There could be no advance color planning, other than the overall selection of colors that Van Gogh had used. I sat at my kitchen table under a skylight, literally surrounded by piles of greens, purples, oranges, golds, and whites."

Begin Drawing, So That You Can Draw 33

Finding Reference Images

Never has it been easier to find images to help us in our efforts to draw. Google and other search engines have all but eliminated our trips to the library. With our laptops or tablets, we can sit in our pajamas at the kitchen table, calling up hundreds and thousands of images to help us draw. We must be careful, of course, to use images in ways that are legal and ethical.

One way to use an image is to copy it explicitly. Images that are in the public domain are available for this kind of use. If you wish to draw a windmill on the prairie and hook that image, you could enter search terms "windmill images public domain." By including the phrase "public domain," we can restrict our search to pieces of art that are free for the taking. Be sure to read the sidebar on copyright (page 78) in the Start with Art chapter, and remember that when you adapt an image explicitly, even if it is in the public domain, it's best to declare up front that the design did not originate with you.

Another way to use the images we find online is to study them as reference images. My mother, Lilly Phillips, loves the little groups of does and fawns that come looking for food and

34 Designed By You

water in her wooded back yard. After munching on the alfalfa and corn she sets out for them and drinking her birdbath dry, they lie down and sleep among the trees behind the house. Of course, she wanted to hook a rug, so she looked online at many photographs of deer in the woods, printing some of them for further study. In the end, with the help of my brother, David, she used several different reference photos to create this composite image to draw on her linen and hook.

Deer, *43" x 21", #8-cut and hand-cut wool and yarn on linen. Designed by David Phillips and Lilly Phillips, and hooked by Lilly Phillips, Council Bluffs, Iowa, 2015.* PETER C. PHILLIPS

Lilly used various reference images she found online, and then asked for help from her son, David, for the drawing. Adaptations of David's pencil sketches appear elsewhere in this book.

Begin Drawing, So That You Can Draw 35

Using Technology for Drawing

Given the profusion of useful programs and apps being created today, it is not possible to list them all. For one thing, more programs, websites, YouTube tutorials, and smartphone apps are being developed every day, and our list would be out of date by the time it was published. There has never been a better time to find assistance in drawing. As art students, we must regularly investigate and share new and helpful products.

Here are two specific suggestions for beginning to use technology, the first of which is to give yourself the treat of online tutorial videos on how to draw. I recently entered search terms something like this: "how to draw older people with wrinkles." A wealth of tutorials resulted from my search, with oral explanations from the teacher and time-lapse photography, showing rather quickly how such a drawing takes shape.

Secondly, one of my teachers, Jayne Hester, recommends Photosketch, a smartphone app that allows us to snap a photo on our phones and transform it to line art with a single click. Here is a tool that literally does the drawing for us! As you begin to look into your technology resources, you will find even more useful tools to help you along on your artistic journey.

Transferring Images to Linen

However we collect or draw our rug designs, we must then find the best way to enlarge and transfer the design from paper to linen. Many beginning rug-hooking books offer in-depth explanations of the transfer methods we can use. There are many, and by trial-and-error, you'll find the right method for you. Though we won't go into detail, here is a quick list of options.

Templates

If the design is fairly simple, we can use butcher paper for drawing to scale our templates of the larger motifs in our design. Then it's a matter of cutting out our templates, placing them on the piece of linen, and tracing around the shapes. Once the motifs are drawn, it's usually easy to freehand the background and detail.

Molly's Rug, *24" x 28", #7- and 8-cut wool on linen. Designed and hooked by Lilly Phillips, Council Bluffs, Iowa, 2016.*
PETER C. PHILLIPS

Lilly's granddaughter, Isabella, was away at college and would soon be getting her own apartment. "I miss Bella," Lilly said, "and I remember how important Molly was to Bella when she was little. Everywhere Bella went, Molly went. So I made her a Molly rug for her new apartment, to remind her of her childhood."

Begin Drawing, So That You Can Draw   37

Tracing Fabric

If your image has been enlarged to the correct size, this method works well, though it requires you to trace your design two, or even three, times. Take your sketchbook to a copy store for the enlargement on paper.

Tracing fabric is transparent, allowing you to see through it as you draw. First, place and pin the transparent tracing fabric on your paper design. With your marker, trace over the lines for your first transfer, from paper to tracing fabric. Remove the tracing fabric from your paper and check to make sure your drawing is complete.

Next, place and pin your tracing fabric to your piece of linen. With a fresh, new marker, trace over the lines again. Go slowly, so that the marker penetrates the thin tracing fabric and marks your linen. Before you remove the tracing fabric from the linen, check to see whether your lines are all visible. Even after you remove the tracing fabric from the linen, it's usually necessary to go over the linen with your marker once more, darkening any faint lines where the marker didn't sufficiently penetrate the tracing fabric.

Light Table or Large Window

For this method, your design must be enlarged to the desired size on paper. Make a trip to the copy store, if enlarging is necessary. Using a light table or a large window will usually shorten the time you need for transferring, as this process requires you to outline with your marker only once. First, tape your paper design on the light table or on the large window. Then tape your linen over the paper on the light table or the window. If the pattern is large, you will need a wide roll of strong tape to hold the weight of it on your window (and you may need to clean your window afterward). With the light bulb or daylight behind it, you may be surprised how clearly your design shows through the linen. Now, take your marker and draw the design on the linen, making sure to transfer every important line. Again, check your work before removing the linen from your table or window.

I was skeptical about this window idea, but once I tried it, I realized how quick and easy it truly is.

Donna Hrkman's Grid-Enlargement Tool

The best person to explain this method is Donna herself, but here is a summary. Over the original design on paper, place a one-inch grid on transparent acetate. Trace your design. Then create a larger grid of perhaps two-inch or three-inch squares so that you can double or triple the size of your design on the linen. Without a light table or any special equipment, you can then transfer your design, square by square. Donna sells an inexpensive tool that makes grid enlargement a breeze.

Transparency and Overhead Projector

To the wonderful methods described above, I would like to add the nearly obsolete machine of our school days, the overhead projector. As modern technology takes over in the schools, these machines can sometimes end up in a Dumpster. Make an inquiry at your local school district and try to purchase a used machine. (A quick online search revealed used machines for $30 to $60, and new ones for $150 and up.) You won't even need a screen, as a 4' x 5' piece of Styrofoam insulation from your local home improvement store will be large enough for most patterns, and you can use straight pins for attaching your linen to the Styrofoam board.

I have found this method the easiest of all ways of transferring paper patterns to linen. Usually, my mom and I wait until we have several patterns to transfer, and we do all of them in a couple of hours. Yes, we have to make a dash to the copy store, but only to reproduce each design at its original size on a transparency (acetate). No enlargement is necessary. The projector does the enlarging part.

You'll need two tables, one against a wall for propping up your screen, the Styrofoam board, and the other table for your projector, a few feet from the board.

Using the Overhead Projector

In my parents' garage, we pinned our linen to a large piece of Styrofoam board, which is lightweight and easy to move. The drawing is far simpler than the resulting rug. Most of the detail is added while hooking.

Draw a square or rectangle on your linen that is the desired size of your pattern--the border within which your design must fit. Hang your linen on the board with pins, making sure that the linen is smooth and wrinkle free. When you place the transparency on the overhead projector, the projected image may be too large or too small to fit into your border. No worries. Simply slide the machine closer to the board or further from the board to adjust the image size. When you have your image centered and focused within the border, take up your marker and begin to draw. Two people can work on a design at once. Many a time, my mom and I have stood to the right and the left of our Styrofoam board, drawing our designs together on linen. The overhead projector stores easily, as does the lightweight board.

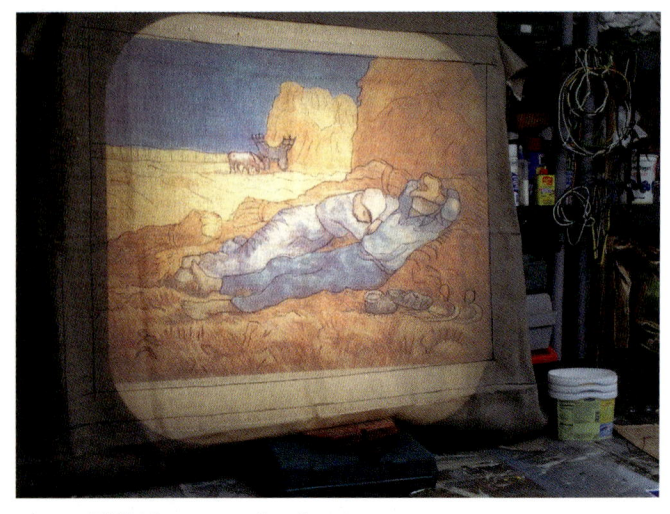

Photo of **Midday** *on overhead projector*

Midday, 45" x 30", #6- through 8.5-cut wool on linen. Adapted from the 1890 Vincent Van Gogh painting of the same name, designed, and hooked by Tamara Pavich, Council Bluffs, Iowa, 2015. PETER C. PHILLIPS

The overhead projector made it very easy to draw this design on linen from a transparency of the original painting, now in the public domain. I added the solid-colored border at the right, with the title of the painting and Van Gogh's initials.

Begin Drawing, So That You Can Draw 39

Drawing Freehand

We all love the saying, "Our linen has two sides." Even if we make a mistake on one side, we can easily flip the linen over and try again. However, too many mess-ups, and we have either made our pattern difficult to use, or we have wasted an expensive piece of linen.

In any case, make one or two or several sketches on paper before marking your linen. Sketching helps you get a grasp of your composition and the proportions of your motifs. Sketch first, before committing marker to linen.

By all means, confident ones, if you are ready to draw freehand on linen, don't be deterred by this suggestion. Sometimes you may feel fairly confident in drawing freehand, but not always. Using some of the other methods described here will make pattern drawing more successful and much clearer and error free. For best results, I usually use one of these methods—making motif templates or using the overhead projector. Even when I use these tools, there are still parts of the design that I fill in by drawing freehand on the linen.

Starting Small and Simple

Eventually, you will have lots of practice under your belt. You'll grow accustomed to using all the tools and technology available to you. And you'll draw your own rug designs of any size. But if you're a new designer, starting small and simple is a surefire way to build confidence.

Chapters 3 through 8 each contain six design ideas. You'll find that the first design idea in each chapter is the simplest to execute, and usually the last design idea is the most advanced or complex. So if you're looking for ways to start small and simple, consider the first design idea in each chapter.

Learning about Composition

Space will not allow us to fully discuss the principles of composition, but please be aware that there is much to learn on this subject. The more you know about composition, the more pleasing your rug designs will be. For instance, you will learn that most successful designs are composed of motifs in odd numbers, not even numbers. You will learn about balance, which is not necessarily the same as symmetry. You will learn about ways of composing your design that lead the viewer's eye into the drawing. Simply learning about composition will probably inspire new rug designs.

Many inexpensive and free resources are available to you. The shelves of my favorite used bookstore hold more books on composition than I can possibly purchase. Online lessons and tutorials abound. And teacher Pris Buttler produced a wonderful little booklet that instructs us in several standard compositions, used by artists since the dawn of time.

Once again, rug hookers today have all the resources we could possibly need to learn about drawing, about composition, and about honing our skills. We have our secret ingredient, wool, and our mantra, "Wool Works Wonders," to bolster our confidence. Please read on and be inspired by the next six chapters, filled with design ideas and wonderful hooked examples. You can draw. It's only a matter of what you'll draw first.

Sunflowers, *17" x 16", #7- and 8-cut wool on linen. Designed and hooked by Ann Eastman, La Vista, Nebraska, 2016.* PETER C. PHILLIPS

Ann had admired hooked rugs for years and finally resolved to begin hooking. She sketched a simple flower design on paper, tweaked it, and then drew it freehand on her piece of linen. It's noteworthy that she had the courage to design and draw her first rug.

Begin Drawing, So That You Can Draw **41**

3

Start with a Style

Accept the many paths to successful artmaking—from reclusive to flamboyant, intuitive to intellectual, folk art to fine art. One of those paths is yours.
—David Bayles and Ted Orland

Amish textile arts are gracefully simple. Panamanian art is strikingly colorful. Victorian art is typically orderly in composition and subdued in terms of color. "Style is the natural consequence of habit," wrote David Bayles and Ted Orland in their inspiring book *Art and Fear*. Cultures can produce an artistic style, with unique artistic traits and sensibilities, because of certain cultural "habits." Similarly, art movements cohere around certain artistic features or habits.

In our first "Start With" chapter, we're using the word "style" in a general sense. There are many kinds of rugs in the world, which have developed out of many different situations and conditions. As we begin a quest for our own style, it's useful to try out a variety of other styles and see which artistic habits attract and inspire us. In this chapter, we offer a choice of six styles that may inspire a rug design of your own.

A naïve style can give us the freedom of children—we can forget about proportion and perspective when we draw. Naïve design is deemed charming precisely because it ignores the rules. A whimsical style allows us to put our imaginations in the driver's seat—or the artist's chair—and see what fantastic images result. If we desire a little structure, a geometric design could be just the thing. We can ground a favorite motif on a grid, or simply feature the colorful geometry itself. One of my first rugs was made in the style of an heirloom, or in other words, I used various techniques to make the rug look old and worn, as though it had survived many decades of use. From the fine-art world, we can borrow the term "impressionism," endowing our chosen image with skewed shapes, altered perspective, and intensified color. And finally, we can peruse arts across the globe and give ourselves an anthropology lesson through designing and hooking a rug derived from another culture.

Of course, the world is full of styles, waiting for us to discover and try them. Classic or modern, simple or complex, indigenous or acquired, consider the world of style your oyster. Open it!

OPPOSITE PAGE: Love's Song, *25" x 36", #2- through 4-cut wool on Scottish burlap. Adapted from a 1920s piece of sheet music. Designed and hooked by Joanne Thomason, Newton, Iowa, 2005.*

Joanne is drawn to designs of the '20s, '30s, and '40s, and she likes to wander antique stores, looking for images to adapt. "I like the swirls and the movement in this design," Joanne said. "This color plan is very close to the sheet music illustration."

43

Design Idea #1: Be Naïve!

*Every child is an artist.
The problem is how to remain an artist once he grows up.*

—Pablo Picasso

Winter Nuthatches, *19" x 28", #8-cut wool on linen. Designed and hooked by Nancy Peterson, Glenwood, Iowa, 2007.*

Notice that the sweet little shapes of the birds are placed on the branches in various poses without regard for realism. All of the elements have been greatly simplified, the key to this charming design. "The inspiration for the rug was a crab apple tree in my backyard," Nancy said. "It is often full of nuthatches throughout the winter. My husband and I love watching them flock to the tree and gobble berries while the ground is covered with snow."

Pull out your sketchbook. Pick up a crayon. Trust your intuition. Imagine a favorite thing. Keep it simple. Draw with joy.

This design idea gives you permission to be a kid again. No need to trouble yourself with the p-words, proportion and perspective. You are a child with a paper and pencil, making your picture. You can't do it wrong. Play around. Draw what you like. A kitty-cat. A willow tree. A bird. A house with a door and a window.

Now you get to choose two or three items from your sketchbook for your rug design. Experts say that odd numbers of motifs are pleasing to the eye, but let's ignore all the rules today. You can't do it wrong. Let your own eye be the judge. If two or four motifs look right to you, then that's your number.

Here's the perfect moment to try templates. Using butcher paper or a brown paper bag, draw the outlines of your motifs to scale, cut them out, and place them on the linen. How do they look together? If one motif seems too large or too small, no problem. Redraw it before marking the linen. (See Chapter 2 for more on templates.)

Now, remember our mantra: Wool Works Wonders. Don't overthink your color plan. Five crayons may be enough for this design. Select five colors, five pieces of wool from your stash, and place them on the linen. You can't do it wrong. Hook your largest motif in a color, and then ask yourself what your eye wants to see next.

A design with only a few simple motifs allows you to play in the background and the border. Make your background interesting by giving it some movement. Will you use one wool or a mixture of wools in your background? And how will you hook it? Perhaps "Lazy Cs and Ss," which give us interesting shapes to contour around until our background is filled. Or try other options: draw puzzle pieces, a wonky grid, or wavy horizontal lines in your background. You can't do it wrong. Ever tried a hit-or-miss border? You might like those short stripes, wavy or straight, distributing your colors nicely around the outside edge.

Naïve designs are not just for the beginner. Some familiar names have made naïve art their chosen style: "It took me four years to paint like Raphael," said Pablo Picasso, "but a lifetime to paint like a child." When life gets too complicated, or for that matter, when hooking becomes a little too challenging, remember that you can always come back to your childlike joy. Be naïve.

Checkers, *12" x 14", #6- to 8-cut on linen. Designed and hooked by Laura Schram, Lincoln, Nebraska, 2015.*

"This rug was adapted from photos of a well-loved cat and the blue Tudor home where my children grew up," Laura said. "My daughter, Melissa Thorne, painted a watercolor of our black and white Manx cat, and that painting was also my inspiration. The brick-colored background, inspired by the brick street laid in 1916 in front of the home, gave a soft antique feel to this rug. The naïve design of the oversized cat was on my list to do for a long time, because the cat was the heart of our home.

"I drew the house and cat on white paper, then used Red Dot tracing fabric to put the design on linen. As I outlined the cat, I shaped it more to my daughter's watercolor design shape. One of most difficult things was adding definition between the legs and body of the cat. I used a string from my linen backing to put a little spark in his eye."

Design Idea #2: A Little Whimsy

Puff the magic dragon lived by the sea . . .

—Peter Yarrow, Puff the Magic Dragon

Feeling Utterly Gorgeous, *18" x 12" (chair back) and 18" x 16" (chair seat), recycled fabrics, mainly t-shirts, and sheep's fleece on hessian. Designed and hooked by Diane Cox, Penzance, Cornwall, 2013.*

"We had a group project to transform an old chair with hooking," Diane said, "and I like hooking faces. This represents an older lady who has realized that real beauty comes from within, from having self-belief, self-esteem, and being comfortable in one's own unique skin.

"I hooked a companion chair representing a young woman with the words 'not yet knowing her beauty' hooked on the seat. I like to place them together in my studio, facing each other, as if they were mother and daughter."

Sometimes the word "whimsy" is mistaken for frivolous or unimportant. Let's refute that notion with some synonyms for whimsical: fanciful, playful, mischievous, curious, eccentric, quirky, outlandish, offbeat, freaky.

What awesome words! Who wouldn't love to draw an offbeat rug design or a freaky one? This style-design idea is like the previous one in that it asks our inner child to come out and play. Thumb through children's storybooks or fairy tale collections to get into the spirit of this exercise. You can always keep it simple: put a smile on a coffee pot or enlarge a ladybug. Give your sense of humor a voice. Let your dreamer-self take over. May one of these quirky ideas intrigue you.

Tall Tale
Did you fold 77 loads of laundry today? Do your tomato plants tower over the rooftops? Are you feeding a whole forest out of three little bird feeders? Embellish a story in your whimsical rug design.

Music as Muse
Consider favorite song lyrics for inspiration. "Lucy in the Sky with Diamonds" would inspire a very different design than "Home on the Range," but wouldn't it be fun to hook heavenly Lucy in the twinkling firmament or let the deer and the antelope play across your pattern?

Yuk It Up
Remember that kid in the back of the classroom who was always making people laugh? Be that kid. If something or someone bores you or gets on your nerves, yuk it up. A nosy neighbor, your messy garage, a traffic jam—give these irksome problems their own humorous rug, and share the laugh with your hooking buddies.

Sketch away, designers. When you have refined a favorite whimsical design in your sketchbook, get it on the linen.

The Firebird, *24½" x 46", #4-, 5-, and 6-cut wool and repurposed sari silk on linen. Designed by Tatiana Tipton and Jane Baty, and hooked by Tatiana Tipton, Ames, Iowa, 2014.*

"The Firebird," Tatiana said, "is an imaginary bird with a large tail. It's a character from Russian fairy tales. It flies at night and has magical powers. Artists have represented the firebird in many different ways. In addition to many examples from graphic arts, there is Igor Stravinsky's ballet, *The Firebird,* with representation both in the music and costume. I was interested in creating a wall hanging using wool and repurposed sari silk, featuring an exotic multicolored bird against a big moon. I had several inspirations as well as help from an artist friend. Combining different textures and colors was challenging, satisfying and fun."

Start with a Style   **47**

Design Idea #3: Go Geo

The possibilities are endless when it comes to geometric hand-hooked rugs.

—Gail Dufresne

Harley, *12" x 12", #6-cut wool on linen. Designed and hooked by Nancy Peterson, Glenwood, Iowa, 2010.*

"My dog, and walking buddy, Harley, inspired the mat," Nancy said, "which was made into a pillow. I took a photo of Harley and copied it in black and white. Then I marked the areas of color that I wanted to hook to make his face reflect his image accurately. The background grid was hooked with two shades of the same color. With the grid, I alternated hooking horizontally and vertically to give it more interest."

Anyone interested in exploring geometric designs must get her hands on the definitive volume, *Geometric Hooked Rugs* by Gail Dufresne. Whatever narrow ideas we may have about the definition of a geometric rug are exploded by the author's wide-ranging imagination. The explanations are helpful and thorough, and the rug photographs are increasingly inspiring.

Perhaps you would like to begin with the simple, classic form of the inch mat to create your first original geometric rug. Drawing the grid with one-inch or two-inch squares is easy enough, allowing a wide or narrow border. Naturally, straight lines are important. Although it's common to use black or a dark color to outline the grid, don't hesitate to change things up. According to Gail, almost any color can be used for the outline. Her book offers endless variations on this simple theme, in which the geometric design itself is the rug's central feature. She has also placed various motifs on her grids—owls, cats, dogs, roosters, and, most memorably, her signature goats and reptiles.

We can also take instruction from quilters who have been doing geometric designs for centuries. The Log Cabin or Nine-Patch can make simple starting points, but look further. Quilting magazines abound, and so do blogs and web sites. Diamond in the Square, Hourglass, Pinwheel, Eight-Point Star, Flying Geese, Courthouse Steps: dozens of quilt designs can become your first geometric rug design. You may be attracted to classics or be inspired to tweak them, but take a moment to read about their history. Log Cabin quilts have a warm fire at their center—a red block in the middle of every quilt block to symbolize the hearth as the center of the home. Some Log Cabin quilts have yellow center blocks to signify a candle in the window. When you hook a quilt pattern, you are participating in an old story with meaning. Investigate that meaning to enhance your hooking pleasure.

Don't be deceived by the simplicity of quilt designs. Even a brief study of quilt patterns reveals the subtle complexity and striking variations that can occur through your uses of color and value.

Finally, the square and the rectangle are not the only geometric shapes available. If you prefer curves to angles, try populating your canvas with circles, ovals, or spirals. Create overlapping shapes or shapes within shapes, whatever pleases your eye. Simple or complex, "go geo" with your next original design.

Log Cabins, *15½" x 23". #7- and 8-cut wool on linen. Designed and hooked by Beth Zerweck-Tembo, Bridgewater, Virginia, 2008.*

"My Charlottesville, Virginia, rug hooking group issued a challenge," Beth said. "We were given an outline of a simple house or cabin and asked to design a rug incorporating it in some way. For some time, I couldn't think of anything appealing to do with this cabin. Meanwhile, in another group in Harrisonburg, Virginia, we were working on rugs with the log cabin quilt design.

"Finally, an inspiration. Why not use the cabin theme from both group challenges, combining a quilt log cabin with the simple cabin shape? To complement the geometric nature of the quilt log cabin, I turned the house into a geometric design element by repeating it and making it part of a side panel. The result was a cabin abstracted enough that when we shared our finished rugs, someone said with surprise that I hadn't used the cabin in my design. I pointed out that in fact I had used it six times!"

Start with a Style

Design Idea #4: Instant Heirloom

Old is the new new.

—*Anonymous*

Trotters, 56" x 21", #8- to 9-cut wool on linen. Designed and hooked by Cathy Stephan, Athens, Wisconsin, 2014.

"This is a reproduction rug," Cathy said, "whose title is unknown to me. I first saw it on an auction web site, then in a book. I was drawn to the simple lines of the horses, birds, and tree and was particularly interested in the neutral textures. The use of light, medium, and dark wools—all values—for the background was quite unusual. The small patches of background were also a fun way to use up leftover wool from other projects, particularly tweeds and herringbones.

"I love wide cuts and did start on the tree with an 8½-cut, but it was too wide for the little branches. The rest of it went in well with tweeds I had been collecting over time. Cool gray wools had never been inspiring to me, but these grays were warm, almost mushroom tans, grays, and browns. The hooking time was happy, and I was finished in three weeks' time, in spite of the size."

What is it about those musty, dusty, sometimes neglected, often mistreated, color-faded, hand-hooked rugs, the decades of tread apparent in their flattened loops, that makes us want to fill our houses with them? No matter what contemporary styles we may try during our rug-hooking evolution, we are still charmed by the dear old rugs. Fortunately, many of these folk art treasures have been preserved in the books of Joel and Kate Kopp, Jessie Turbayne, and others. We can still find them in antique stores, usually hidden under tables or rolled up in a corner, waiting for a rug-lover to rescue them. Each was once new. Each was the product of an imagination, a hand, and a hook pulling loops.

We can adopt the style of antique rugs by mimicking a number of their features. Authors Barbara Carroll and Cynthia Norwood have published excellent books filled with techniques for creating an antique look. The goal of my first-ever rug-hooking workshop was to create a brand new "heirloom rug," and my teacher, Janice Lee, instructed us about tearing our strips rather than cutting, hooking in straight lines, mimicking fugitive color, creating patchy backgrounds, and outlining or echoing our motifs. We even learned techniques that would make our brand new rugs look stained or worn. With an almost endless supply of wool on hand, we students imagined what our rugs would look like if we ran out of an important color and had to make do with a less than perfect match. And oh, how we loved our new-old rugs.

You can study antique rugs in books, in museums, in antique stores, or online. Searching the phrase "antique hooked rugs" yields hundreds of beautiful images. Best not to make an explicit adaptation if you are not certain that the artist has died more than 70 years ago, but find a few favorite examples and study their features. Use your sketchbook to develop your design, and then hook your way to the comfort and beauty of an heirloom rug.

Kopp Floral, *34" x 37½", #8-cut on linen. Designed (with help from friends) and hooked by Tamara Pavich, Council Bluffs, Iowa, 2009.* PETER C. PHILLIPS

Even before my first workshop, my hooking friends used to gather and draw rugs together, often using templates for the motifs. That was the case with this rug, so I can't take credit for doing all the drawing myself. We helped each other draw.

The faded scrolls and the mixture of dark background colors, hooked in straight lines, were what attracted me to this design, shown in the famous book by Joel and Kate Kopp, American Hooked and Sewn Rugs. The caption of the rug photo indicated that the original designer would surely have been deceased more than 70 years ago; therefore, the design is in the public domain. Even so, I call this rug Kopp Floral to acknowledge that it is not my original design, but a reproduction of an antique from a well-known folk art book.

Start with a Style 51

Design Idea #5: Impressionism

*If I paint a wild horse, you might not see the horse . . .
but surely you will see the wildness!*

—Pablo Picasso

In the late nineteenth century, an artist had to abide by the rules of the art establishment or pay a high price. Those artists who gave birth to the impressionist movement became famous by way of ridicule. The very name, impressionism, was coined by an art critic who expressed his disgust for Claude Monet's painting entitled *Impression: Sunrise*, comparing it to wallpaper.

Nowadays, that's just water under Monet's infamous bridge. We are so comfortable with and appreciative of impressionist art today that it's hard to imagine a time when it could have been publicly disparaged.

Think of Van Gogh's *Starry Night*, perhaps his most famous painting. You'll recall the whirling, swirling night sky on that canvas, with the tiny orderly village below. Rather than treating a scene or a subject in the more classical style, impressionists like Van Gogh attempt to infuse the work with their own vision. They hope to give the viewer an experience of seeing the subject through the painter's eyes. While classically trained artists made many studies and careful sketches of a subject before laboring to produce the realistic masterwork, impressionist painters would paint much more quickly. In the last 70 days of Van Gogh's life, he experienced an incredible burst of creativity, producing one or more canvases per day. Many of those are now considered his most valuable works, some valued at more than $100 million.

When you create an impressionistic design, you are depicting what you see and also, perhaps, how it makes you feel. According to the mood of a scene or subject, you might play looser with color, using pure or unmixed colors that reflect emotional associations, rather than trying to be completely faithful to realism. The forms don't have to be realistic either. You can distort a body, exaggerate a face, smooth a landscape, illuminate a flower, in ways that show your particular feelings and evoke them in your viewer.

In my humble opinion, the materials we use as rug hookers and the look of our finished works are particularly well suited to impressionism. Select your subject, something that draws your gaze and holds it. Is it the scribble of black branches outside your window? Long shadows before the sun goes down? A delicate arc of bleeding hearts in your garden? Try drawing and hooking your subject or scene in an impressionistic style. Give your viewers a glimpse of the world through your eyes.

OPPOSITE PAGE: Native Prairie, *20" x 45", #8-cut wool, sari silk, and yarn on monk's cloth. Designed and hooked by Holly McMillan, Roca, Nebraska, 2013.*

"My group decided to try hooking in the style of Deanne Fitzpatrick, who hooks landscapes in a very impressionistic way," Holly said. "I have always been partial to the Nebraska sand hills with their many colors of grasses and wildflowers. So the subject matter was just a great match for our group challenge.

"The group wanted to use lots of varying materials that would add texture and interest. We put all of our fibers on a big table so others could try out whatever they liked. My take-home pearl was that I really like mohair yarn, which can be worked in between two regular rows of hooking to add interest.

"We had tossed around the idea of traveling to take a workshop, but the expense and time required made it difficult for our group. I think our alternative of this stay-at-home adventure worked perfectly."

ABOVE: Robin's Egg Blues, *16" x 16", #6-cut and hand-cut wool and sari silk on linen. Adapted from* Nesting III, *encaustic wax on board by Rosemary Clarke Young. Designed and hooked by Linda Smith, Kingston, Ontario, 2014.*

"I was immediately drawn to Nesting III," Linda said, "the beautiful jewel-like colors and the movement in this impressionistic piece. Rosemary's painting is sweet and small, only six inches square. I relied on sari silk in my rug to mimic the shine of the encaustic technique Rosemary used for the original piece. This project made me move away from my mantra that rugs need to live on the floor."

Start with a Style 53

Design Idea #6: Anthropology Lesson

*Though we travel the world over to find the beautiful,
we must carry it with us or we find it not.*

—Ralph Waldo Emerson

African Bird, *16" round, #6- and 8-cut on linen. Designed and hooked by Beth Zerweck-Tembo, Bridgewater, Virginia, 2008.*

"I have long been attracted to the abstract and offbeat ways animals, birds, fish, and reptiles are depicted in African decorative art," Beth said. "Typically these figures are symbolic and stylized with some feature exaggerated or distorted to emphasize a characteristic. Many of these traditional design elements go back centuries yet often seem so modern and avant-garde.

"*African Bird* is my first rug design. I liked that the bird was simple yet had an active pose and interesting geometric patterns. Most African art adorns functional items used in everyday life (pottery, textiles, leather goods, baskets), so I decided to put him on something with a practical use, a round chair pad. Animals and other wildlife are found abundantly in African art. The beauty and function of the art reveal much about the heart and spirit of the people who created it."

Whether or not we can afford to get on a plane and explore other cultures in person, we can certainly learn a lot by exploring the art of cultures across the world. Ancient architecture, Celtic designs, Hawaiian petroglyphs, Egyptian cave paintings, folk textile arts, or our own imaginative interpretations of artifacts: all of these ideas can be studied, designed, and hooked. While making something beautiful, we may also deepen our understanding of another culture and appreciate its art.

Regardless of how much you have traveled, books can be your windows to art around the world. I recently purchased *A Treasury of Indian Folk Textiles* by Carol Summers, and I can hardly look away from its pages of intricate geometric designs and charming folk-art illustrations embroidered on fabric. The colors are deeply saturated and rich. Although I may never visit India, I hope to learn something by studying the rich heritage of Indian folk artists.

Beth Tembo lived in Zambia for almost five years. "I admired Kuba weavings I saw for sale at markets," she said. "On a visit there a few years ago, I finally bought a few. I thought it would be fun to design a Kuba-inspired pattern for a hooked rug, because I find their primitive geometric designs so appealing. The colors range from bright and varied to natural or monochromatic. African design is often considered primitive, but it can be very sophisticated. Kuba cut-pile embroidery weavings, for instance, often appear haphazard. But upon closer study you can see that the artists have a highly developed sense of geometric design."

Debra Walland designed her rug, *Praise House*, while living on Hilton Head Island. "The native islanders," Debra said, "the Gullah people, are descendants of slaves brought from West Africa because of their skill in farming. Because they were somewhat isolated on the island, they have been able to keep alive their unique culture. This is becoming more difficult now with the resort community growing around them, but they have a strong pride in their heritage."

Debra incorporated cultural elements into this rug: the music of praise emanating from the house of worship, shown through vibrant bands of color, and the visually interesting background of an indigo-dyed batik. (*Praise House* is on page 57).

As you gather hooking ideas, roam the world in your imagination and assign yourself an anthropology lesson in rug design.

Africanus, *28" x 40", #4-through 8-cut wool on linen. Designed and hooked by Pris Buttler, Gainesville, Georgia, 2015.*

When joining in a group challenge to hook a rug in the style of a tarot card, Pris designed this gorgeously detailed piece.

Start with a Style **55**

(Anthropology continued)

Kuba Quadrilateral, 20" x 23", #4-cut wool on linen, inspired by Kuba weaving and embroidery. Designed and hooked by Beth Zerweck-Tembo, Bridgewater, Virginia, 2015.

"I have long been intrigued with African textiles," Beth said. "The center part of my rug is inspired by several cut-pile embroidery weaving designs. I just made up the abstract shapes in the left and right borders, but they are inspired by shapes embroidered on Kuba weavings. The bottom three shapes on the left border are actually my initials, BZT.

"I hooked my whole rug in the same direction, up and down, except the yellow outline of the diamonds, to give it a look closer to a weaving. Because I do like asymmetry and not having everything the same, I did hook one diamond in the opposite direction, and another one outlined in dark purple. I especially like the background fill between the diamonds and how the color flows from dark to light with reds, oranges, and purples. Most Kuba weavings of similar design don't do this, but I saw a few that had a mix of dark and light in between diamonds and thought that would bring some interest to the piece."

56 Designed By You

Praise House, *22" x 20", #6-cut wool on linen. Designed and hooked by Debra Walland, Bluffton, South Carolina, 2009.*

Debra designed this rug while living on Hilton Head Island. *"The Gullah are very church centered, and their ancestors combined the Christian faith of the missionaries, mostly Methodist, with their own African rites. Music, dancing, and drumming were integral to their worship. The praise house was a simple community meeting place and house of worship prior to the modern churches.*

"Their traditions continue today, although hand clapping has often replaced drumming. I had hoped to capture the energy of joyful praise and worship coming from these churches without a sense of time. I initially planned to include a moss-draped oak tree to give a sense of place, but decided instead on the background of an indigo-dyed batik. The Gullah are known for batik dyeing. Indigo was a common plantation crop here."

4

Start with Color

Mere color, unspoiled by meaning, and unallied with definite form, can speak to the soul in a thousand different ways.

—Oscar Wilde

Dad, 11" x 14", #3-, 4-, 6-, and 8-cut wool on linen. Designed and hooked by Luci Bolding, Omaha, Nebraska, 2015.

In her class with Donna Hrkman, Luci began with color, knowing she wanted to do an unconventional portrait of her father. "The colors were inspired by a painting I had seen," Luci said. "I had an enlarged black and white photo of Dad, and Donna had me use colored pencils to identify the shapes of the shadows on his face. I mapped it out and transferred those shapes to the rug. Dad lives in Florida, and this rug reminds me of our fun times on vacation there. And, of course, I love my dad and this portrait of him in his Florida home."

We sometimes get into the habit of thinking of rug hooking like coloring with crayons. We begin with a design or a pattern—the page in our coloring book—and we fill in parts of the design with our wool colors. We think of color as the second step in the creative process, not the first.

But have you ever been taken with a color or a combination of colors? I was suddenly swept off my feet by various greens placed next to each other. I didn't have a design in mind, but I wanted to hook blue-greens and yellow-greens side-by-side. So I drew some simple shapes--the lines barely mattered to me. I just needed some design to hold my blue, green, and yellowish loops near each other. (See *Yin-Yang Chair Seat* on page 8.)

Sometimes exciting designs begin with color inspiration

Zodiac, *30" diameter, various yarns on rug warp. Designed and hooked by Kay LeFevre, Windsor, Ontario, 2012.*

Kay hooked this piece for a girlfriend in Michigan, who was a collector of zodiac things. Using clip art for the motifs, she hooked in the rainbow of color, making a circuit of the color wheel. "I added the sun and moon in the center," Kay said, "because I love the symbolism of the earth tied to the celestial. I hooked the sun and moon with Martha Stewart glitter eyelash yarn to make them glow."

first and the "picture" or the rug design evolves from our love of color. Luci Bolding first decided to try a new type of portrait with patches of brilliant color identifying the values in her father's face. Kay LeFevre designed her *Zodiac* rug around the spectrum of the whole color wheel.

These six design ideas will encourage our novice rug designers to play with their favorite colors, to enhance color with outlining, and to try out a brand new box of crayons. Our more advanced design ideas suggest incorporating the four essential qualities of dark, light, dull, and bright; restricting a color palette to a single chroma; and finally doing without color altogether by working with black, white, gray, and other neutrals.

Design Idea #1: Your Color Runner

*Why do two colors, put one next to the other, sing?
Can one really explain this?*

—Pablo Picasso

While pictorials, portraits, and landscape designs usually demand concentration, hooking a colorful runner leaves your mind free to meditate on your favorite wool colors.

Your design can be as simple as you like. On your piece of linen, draw the long rectangle of your floor or table runner. Add a border, narrow or wide. You can divide your rectangle into color blocks, or put color blocks into your border. Five, seven, or nine simple shapes (try circles, spiral swirls, triangles, or primitive bird shapes) placed along the length of the rectangle will make a lovely piece. Or draw a curving vine that runs down the middle, adding simply shaped leaves and berries at regular intervals.

Follow Cathy Stephan's example and allow your runner design to be blessedly simple, so that color can be your primary focus. Cathy's *Navajo Runner* uses wide-cut wool and mostly straight-line hooking, with a few curves and beading for visual interest.

Your walls, floors, and furnishings already reflect your favorite colors. Select colors that would bring together the color scheme of your chosen room. If the room is overwhelmingly teal, for instance (like some of my rooms), add contrast with the complement of salmon, orange, or rust. If the room is subdued, with muted tones, punch it up with brighter hues.

In your stash, you will certainly have your favorite wool colors left over from other rugs. Five or even three colors is plenty, because you can use several versions of each color, lighter and darker shades, both dulls and brights, textures and flannels. Perhaps some leftover noodles will find a place in this design. Gather your wools, cut some strips, and go to it.

Contrast is your friend. As you meditate on the pleasing colors of your loops, think about how warm colors sing next to cool ones, how satisfying it is to alternate lighter and darker values, and how a few rows of dull color invite the introduction of something brighter.

Notice that Cathy Stephan's borderless *Compass Runner* employs brighter colors and textures in the compass motifs, while her background is made up of dull medium-value browns in a hit-or-miss design. Oh, the leftover noodles that could disappear into this interesting background! Cathy's motifs are outlined in black, defining the colors and textures, and her binding is whipped with black to echo the black outlining.

Whether you're just beginning to design or you've been designing for years, give yourself the gift of hooking a simple runner and relax into a meditation on color.

Compass Star Runner, *14" x 86", #8- and 8.5-cut wool on linen. Designed and hooked by Cathy Stephan, Athens, Wisconsin, 2015.*

"This is an antique reproduction rug. The original had much more of a golden brown tone with tan dominant in the background. I decided I had to have a better color plan than that one, though it was probably done with what was available from old clothing at the time. I admired the stripy background and loved the dark (but not too dark) outline of the star segments. Since I have new wools as well as old to choose from—a much different stash than the woman who hooked the original—I chose a tweedy wool for each star to give it visual appeal, and then other more colorful wools. I used mainly leftover worms for the background, but even this large rug did not seem to reduce the bushels of worms I have collected over the years. It is used on our eight-foot farmhouse table in the kitchen."

Navajo Runner, *26" x 61", #9.5-cut wool on linen. Designed and hooked by Cathy Stephan, Athens, Wisconsin, 2012.*

"I have always loved Navajo rugs," Cathy said, "and wanted to try my hand at a design with a woven look. I liked the look of straight rows with some curves for interest. These fall colors are somewhat brighter than my usual muted palette. The eye is always drawn to the lightest areas and the dirty white took the eye to the center. The beaded lines carried the eye around the whole rug. Instead of adding too many colors, I take the orange, for example, and find other wools that have some orange in them. An occasional tweed or herringbone keeps the colors interesting to look at. Using the same wool too many times leaves the viewer bored (the hooker, too!). I used a lot of textures that read as tweedy, because the eye loves pixels of color and light even more than great solid-looking color. Whenever I was stumped as to what color should go next, I used neutrals. Browns, taupes, warm grays--all extend your color palette without crowding the color plan."

Design Idea #2: The Stained Glass Effect

Van Gogh's use of black outlines has rightly been attributed to the influence of Gauguin.

—Debora Silverman

Day Lily #1, 9" x 9 ¾", #4-cut wool on linen. Designed and hooked by Trish Johnson, Toronto, Ontario, 2000.

Outlining with dark values makes beautiful colors even more beautiful. If you doubt it, look at a leaded glass window. I go weak in the knees over prairie glass and other designs of the Craftsman period. Often the lovely colors of the glass draw the eye, but it's the lead, the consistent dark outlining of those panes of colored glass, that endows the colors with their impact.

One of the first things I learned as I began to adapt a painting of Vincent Van Gogh was the importance of the narrow black outline that defines every figure in the painting. As I began that rug, my first task was to cut narrow strips of black-brown wool. Without it, I certainly could have hooked the two farmers, their shoes, their scythes, and their haystacks, but I wouldn't have captured the look of a Van Gogh painting—not without the outline. (See *Midday* on page 39.)

The simple decision to outline with black changes the look of a rug, creating a well-defined picture, and—when the outlining is used consistently as a feature—a distinctly stylized design. My teacher, Pris Buttler, explained this to me in a workshop, in which I asked her to help me with an original design featuring a great blue heron, framed by cattails.

Pris instructed me to draw the elements simply, with curving, horizontal bands of color in the lake where my heron serenely stood. The figures of the heron and the cattails, every leaf and stem, even the ripples on the water's surface, would be outlined in a very dark blue. With Pris's guidance, my wildlife tribute to Wendell Berry began to take on the look of a stylized art poster. (See *The Peace of Wild Things* on pages 74-75.)

Day Lily #2, *10½" x 10", #4-cut wool on linen. Designed and hooked by Trish Johnson, Toronto, Ontario, 2000.*

With her Day Lily rugs, Trish set out to explore a complementary color scheme, and the stained-glass design amplified her pleasing choices. "I chose the day lily for its cheerful orangeness and dyed the background blue because blue is the complement of orange. I chose a greenish blue in particular because the orange is a yellowish orange." Trish also dyed the green for the leaves.

Melancholie, *11" x 14", #4-cut wool on linen. Designed by Pearl McGown and hooked by Val Flannigan, Kelowna, British Columbia, 2010.*

"I was assigned this pattern for my teaching accreditation," Val said. "I was to teach stained glass. The biggest consideration was color. I chose to do it in a fairly traditional color scheme. Then I wanted to do another one using a completely different color scheme. At that time, the movie Avatar was popular, so I chose to do a blue face. Once this was decided, I chose colors based on the color wheel, complementary color for the leading and used an analogous scheme for the other elements. I did have to be aware of values for definition between the elements."

To give this design idea a try, draw a geometric pattern, a botanical design, or even a simple landscape, in which black outlining will be used throughout the rug. Your design can be complex and elaborate or simple and elegant. Observe how your colors become more striking when outlined in black.

If you like to use the color wheel, try any scheme. Whether you employ complements, analogous colors, or a triad, the colors will appear more vibrant when you outline with a dark value. And by outlining with black, you'll be joining the ranks of Arts & Crafts designers, stained glass artists, and Vincent Van Gogh himself.

For the most part, this book is filled with rugs designed by the rug hooker; however, we couldn't resist Val's treatment of this McGown pattern. It demonstrates the effect that outlining has on color.

Start with Color 63

Design Idea #3: Adopt a Palette

The world is your kaleidoscope.
—James Allen

Hope I, 18½" x 18½", #6-, #7-, and #8-cut wool on linen. Adapted with permission from the collage of the same name by Elizabeth St. Hilaire Nelson. Designed and hooked by Tamara Pavich, Council Bluffs, Iowa, 2013.

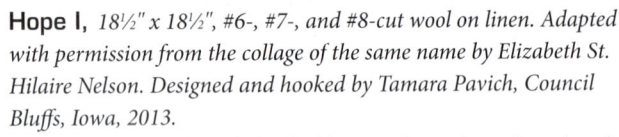

My hookings imitated Elizabeth's marvelous color palette, but they didn't really look like collages. That's why my teacher, Anita White, suggested making the border look like a collage, as a further tribute to Elizabeth and the medium she uses. I had fun using a variety of purple wools to create the irregular shapes in an attempt to mimic the look of torn pieces of paper.

Hope II, 18½" x 18½", #6-, #7-, and #8-cut wool on linen. Adapted with permission from the collage of the same name by Elizabeth St. Hilaire Nelson. Designed and hooked by Tamara Pavich, Council Bluffs, Iowa, 2014.

"I don't know how Elizabeth does it," Tamara said, "but somehow she captures an attitude or endearing quality of the animals and birds in her art. I found this sweet robin irresistible. I'm happy with the bird, and not so much with the nest, but I have learned so much from Elizabeth, about art and about generosity."

When I began attending workshops,

I sometimes heard these words: "Those aren't my colors." Thinking about that statement, I began to assess my own color affinities. I was a fierce lover of teal and all greens. Dirty pinks and rusty reds showed up in all my rugs. Like everyone, I had my favorite colors, but did I harbor prejudices against others? Were there colors that I avoided? Well, yes. Yellow—usually not for me. Purple—in small, dull doses only. Fire-engine red—never.

As I thumbed through *Rug Hooking* magazine, mind you, I would find gorgeous yellow and purple and fire-engine red rugs. But as much as I might admire those colors in the creations of another hooker, I never selected them myself.

Due to a growing alarm that I was cutting myself off from entire worlds of color, I started playing a little game called "Adopt a Palette." For my first monochromatic, I could have selected my familiar greens. But to broaden my color horizons, I chose purple instead. From pale lavenders to deep violets, I used nothing but the many shades and tints of purple in that rug. And by the time it was finished, purple and I had become friends. (See *Dance in Violet* on page 70).

Next, I fell head-over-heels in love with Elizabeth St. Hilaire Nelson's songbird collages. With her permission, I made a date with her dazzling color palettes, but my stash was sadly inadequate. I ordered blindingly bright orange from Nola Heidbreder and intense, saturated blues from Anita White, in order to adapt and hook Elizabeth's pretty birds, adopting her palette.

Once I'd hooked those adaptations, there was no going back. Loop by brilliant loop, my perception of the color spectrum had been permanently broadened.

Most recently, I discovered an abstract painting, *Stones on the Bottom*, by Oregon artist Lesley Strother, and a new

Stones on the Bottom,
37" x 23", #6- through 8-cut wool on linen. Adapted with permission from the painting of the same name by Lesley Strother. Designed and hooked by Tamara Pavich, Council Bluffs, Iowa, 2014.

The painting is owned by my friends in Oregon, and they helped me get in touch with Lesley to ask permission to hook this rug. I bought almost all the wool for this rug, because it introduced me to a new palette. Thank goodness I began it in a workshop with Pris Buttler and finished it on my own. My rug is brighter and sharper than the original painting. Some of Lesley's nuances were beyond my talents and beyond my stash.

palette that mixed bright and dull colors—almost every color on the spectrum—in ways I had never seen. With Lesley's permission to adapt, I went looking for wool, finding everything I needed at Janice Lee's Rug Hooking Store. I was off and running with a newly adopted palette.

Do you find yourself using the same colors of the same intensity? Are you envious of friends who are taking greater chances with their color choices? Maybe it's time for you to play a round of Adopt a Palette. Be brave. It's a one-rug risk. After several experiments, I found that what I had once labeled "bright" had become something of mid-intensity. Consequently, I have opened up space on my wool shelves for my new definition of bright. And yellow. And purple. And fire-engine red.

Start with Color

Design Idea #4: The Contrasts of DLDB

You don't notice the light without a bit of shadow.
—Libba Bray

Romp In Peace, 28" x 36", #8-cut wool on linen. Designed and hooked by Tamara Pavich, Council Bluffs, Iowa. 2010.

This is my Borzoi, Mythka, who died in 1999. She used to love to go for midnight romps in the cemetery. If Pris Buttler had not insisted on the addition of acid green to this rug, it would have been light, dark, and very dull indeed. PETER C. PHILLIPS

Learning the importance of balancing these four elements—dark, light, dull, and bright—is a big step in our progress as rug designers. It is the yin and the yang of rug hooking. It's not that we need equal parts of all four, but that each element must be present in the rug.

Dark and light—that's the easier part. Early in our rug-hooking educations, we learn that contrast between lighter and darker values makes for a clear picture or design. We learn to separate our wools into lights, mediums, and darks, and we create contrast between our motifs and our background color, or else we could not distinguish the elements in the design.

It's the other aspect of color—called intensity, the balance of dullness and brightness in our rugs—that we sometimes overlook. When it comes to intensity, rug-hookers often fall into one of two schools of thought. I was once a hooker of exclusively dull colors, and in fact, my favorite wools had likely been smudged with gray or brown dye to dull the chroma. Oh, how I adored my muddy greens, rusty reds, and charcoal grays. I still do. But today when I look at some of my early rugs, I feel that something is missing.

In recent years, I have attempted more contemporary designs and art adaptations, trying new colors, some of them pretty loud. As I enjoy colors of higher intensity or brightness, I sometimes forget to include duller ones—a different version of the same problem! In a relentlessly bright design, the viewer can barely distinguish what is important. Without shadow, there's no sunshine.

> **TIP**
>
> "Poison" is the color that sparks up your rug and makes it more interesting. This was once called the "discord," the exciting color note that adds visual interest by interrupting harmony. Sometimes, the poison color will seem incongruous with the color plan, but it can be the antidote to the too-harmonious color scheme.

Pris Buttler gave me an excellent lesson on the subject. As I hooked my rug of exclusively dull colors, she casually dropped small pieces of zingy bright wool onto my canvas. "Add some of that," she said. She called it "spark" or "poison," and it terrified me. But as I worked acid green into my peaceful cemetery scene, the whole rug started to come alive. I used perhaps two dozen strips of that green. It made my rug sing.

Here's your chance to learn from Pris. Whatever rug you choose to design, get your DLDB on! Is the design primarily dull? Fabulous, but give it the contrast of a zingy bit of poison. Is your rug design primarily bright? Brilliant, but don't neglect to put in your shadow colors, too. Even a little bit of contrast will take you a long way.

Flower Clouds, *15½" x 18", #6-cut wool on linen. Adapted from the painting of the same name by Odilon Redon. Designed and hooked by Lou Ann Ayres, Papillion, Nebraska, 2014.*

"To get the feeling of movement in the clouds," Lou Ann said, she hooked them in the antigodlin style. "As I worked with color, I realized to gain form and realism, I needed to have the contrasts of dark and light, bright and dull. The style of hooking, as well as these contrasts, created the effect of rolling clouds. Once the vision was developed, this moved very quickly and smoothly, as you could feel the rolling of the clouds as you hooked."

Design Idea #5: A Color Family

Blue is my world since I'm without you.

—Marty Robbins

Courthouse Steps, *four mats, 7½" square, #8-cut wool on linen. Designed and hooked by Anita White, Overland Park, Kansas, 2014.*

"I hooked these little mats to show the four definitions of monochromatic in hooked quilt blocks," Anita said. "I felt that blue would work the best."

Imagine living with one color family for the period it takes to finish a small mat. That is what my friends and I did last year when we hooked our first monochromatic rugs. Anita chose blue, a color family familiar to her. Holly chose yellow, living for weeks with the darkest olive shades up through her brightest buttery tints. And I chose to spend a month with violets, dark and light, dull and bright.

Hooking a monochromatic rug allows us to explore all versions of a color and yet render our design in a single hue. You may use this design idea to indulge your love of a favorite color family or to get more comfortable with one you don't use very often. The benefits of this project are many, but as teacher Marjorie Duizer says, "The best thing that students take away is a much better handle on values. They learn how to achieve highlights and shadows without depending on different colors to guide them."

Virtually any design can be rendered as a monochromatic. If the plan is to adapt a photograph, it can be enlarged and converted to grayscale for a monochromatic visual guide. Florals and paisley designs typically feature a variety of colors, making them interesting choices for a monochromatic experiment.

Here are three color schemes to choose from when designing your experiment with a color family.

A Single Hue in Many Tints and Shades

Using the strictest definition of the term, monochromatic art uses a single chroma—one blue, not a variety of blues—with many values of that one hue. Adding white to the hue is called tinting. Adding black is called shading. But only tinted and shaded versions of a single color may be used in a true monochromatic scheme.

Neighbors on the Color Wheel

Our second definition of monochromatic expands from a single place on the color wheel to two or three places. Anita's quilt block introduces blue green alongside blue. This scheme is harmonious, while offering greater variation in color than the true monochrome. We call this a tight analogous scheme.

Chimney Rock, *23" x 23", #7- and 8-cut wool and wool yarn on linen. Designed and hooked by Holly McMillan, Roca, Nebraska, 2014.*

Holly spent much of her childhood in the sand hills of Nebraska, and this towering image of Chimney Rock awash in the sunrise is part of her series of Nebraska-inspired rugs. For help with color, Holly turned to her mom, a master quilter, who suggested the Ultimate 3-in-1 Color Tool by Joen Wolfrom. This tool provides the full spectrum of tints and shades for every color.

Adding Neutrals

This definition of monochromatic, often used in pottery and other visual arts, includes works that employ one hue plus the neutral "ground color." For our purposes, neutrals are black, white, gray, and some shades of brown. Sometimes the chroma is dominant, and sometimes the neutrals are dominant. So long as there is just one chroma, the scheme is monochromatic.

Select your subject matter and draw the design. Select a single color. Select your monochromatic scheme from those defined above. And see what you learn from the time you spend with one color family.

(A Color Family continued)

Dance in Violet, 30" x 21½", #6- through 8-cut wool and wool yarn on linen. Adapted with permission from Michael Corlew's award-winning photograph "Dancing Cranes." Designed and hooked by Tamara Pavich, Council Bluffs, Iowa, 2014.

I knew from the beginning that I wanted to hook the silhouettes of the cranes in blue violet and that I would do the water and reeds in red violet. I called on Anita White to dye almost all of the wool. I find it interesting to imagine what effect would have been achieved by a different choice of analogous hues. What effect would oranges and red oranges have? How would greens and yellow greens change this picture? For me, the purple hues cast this as an evening scene, and the purples have a calming effect on the energetic poses of the dancing birds, almost as if they are settling down to rest.

Sarah, *15" x 29", #2-cut wool on rug warp. Adapted from a photograph by Ed Flories. Designed and hooked by Lois Morris, Rawdon, Quebec, 2000.*

Lois dyed blue swatches in 45 different values to achieve the effect she wanted in this true monochrome. She considers this portrait of her granddaughter her "most satisfying project yet."

Start with Color 71

Design Idea #7: Straying Off the Color Wheel

Gray is the color of an elephant and a mouse,
And a falling apart house.
It's fog and smog, fine print and lint,
It's a hush and the bubbling of oatmeal mush.

—Mary O'Neill, Hailstones and Halibut Bones

With a rainbow of color on our wool shelves, it may seem strange to wander off the color wheel into worlds of gray and neutrals. But this book is a catalogue of explorations, and one way to design around color is to do without it entirely.

Art without color spans all of art history, from Michelangelo's sketches to Picasso's *Don Quixote*, from Ansel Adams's photography to graphic modern art. Among other benefits, achromatic pieces give an artist the freedom to work without the distraction of color. Though we may think that without color a rug could become either too stark or too drab to be appealing, the opposite is true. We can actually achieve high-contrast, graphic designs or a muted and mellow impression with low contrast, such as we often see in primitive schemes. As you imagine creating a design to be hooked without color, consider these ideas and effects.

Structure and Contrast

The use of black and white can emphasize the structure of a scene. It can create a minimalist effect and/or demonstrate the complexity of line, as in Roslyn Logsdon's *Charlotte Reflections*.

Black and White Photography

An adaptation of a photo rendered in black and white can age the image, lending a sense of nostalgia and reminding the viewer of a time when color photography was not readily available. Susan Jankowski adapted her own photograph of her mother's hand, hooking a rug using many different gray values to achieve a realistic image.

The Look of Heirloom Rugs

In the old days, primitive rug hookers often had few wool colors in the rag basket to choose from. Using a lower contrast, achromatic color scheme helps us mimic the look of heirloom rugs. The use of dark and light shades of gray and other neutrals can put a greater emphasis on the textured wools that were often used in early primitives. (See Cathy Stephan's *Trotters* on page 50.)

Achromatic Subject Matter

Sometimes the subject we want to hook has very little or no color, in which case, using an achromatic palette is actually realistic while also achieving some of the other effects described here.

Charlotte Reflections, *17 ½" x 23", #3-cut wool on linen. Designed and hooked by Roslyn Logsdon, Laurel, Maryland, 2004.*

"Many years ago," Roslyn said, "I did a hooking of a window in an old house with a reflection of a tree. Some ideas are not new, but disappear and return at another time. Walking down the street in Charlotte, during an ATHA Biennial in that town, I looked up at a glass building and was amazed to see all the patterns reflected in the windows. The windows became a geometric design. The only colors needed were whites, grays, and blacks. The design became a puzzle of movements and not a building at all. Using one color expands one's search for materials, but soon you discover how many variations exist."

Mom's Hand, *24" x 22", #3- and 4-cut wool on rug warp. Adapted from a photograph. Designed and hooked by Susan Jankowski, Neenah, Wisconsin, 2005.*

"Back in my college days, for a photography class I took a photograph of my mom's hand," Susan said. "Some years later, when she had passed away, my sister and I were given her hooking supplies. With encouragement from my sister, we enrolled in a rug hooking class at our local technical college. Immediately, we were hooked. Our only regret was that we wished we could have hooked with our mother when she was around. That is when I decided to hook her hand, doing what she loved to do and what had now become our passion.

"I choose to hook in black and white because it makes you concentrate on what you see without distraction of color. I have received many compliments on the realism. This my second hooked rug, and I hope that my mom would have liked it."

Start with Color

5

Start with Art

Only those with no memory insist on their originality.

—Coco Chanel

Here's a fact. Writers read voraciously. Fashion designers scrutinize each other's work. Musicians listen astutely to songs and scores of other songwriters and composers. In short, artists immerse themselves in art—not just their own art, but in the work of the masters, in the creations of their contemporaries, and in countless other seemingly unrelated media and images all around them. Artists are tuned in to the world—or rather, the many worlds—of art.

By this time, having reached the fifth chapter of this book, I hope you have accepted the idea that you are an artist. You may qualify the term, call yourself a fledgling artist, a folk artist, a wanna-be artist, and that's okay. But adopt the habit of other artists like yourself: cultivate an insatiable curiosity about painting, photography, sculpture; techniques, methods, tools; composition, color, perspective. Become an art omnivore!

There are countless ways to give yourself a steady diet of art inspiration, and this chapter will go into greater detail about six particular ways that your original rug designs can emerge from your study and practice of art. But every rug hooker should be aware of the museums and galleries in her town, state, or province, and visit occasionally or regularly. Make a lunch date with a friend who hooks, and walk slowly through a gallery together, scanning for images that move you. Go to a wide variety of shows and exhibits--take in a quilt show, visit folk art displays, or check out collections of retro art posters. Inspiration may come from anywhere.

Used bookstores are incredible resources for quality books on art periods, styles, and individual artists. You could find a treatise on the post-impressionist period, a volume of works by Amadeo Modigliani, and a book on artfully composing your painting (or in your case, rug), all for under $15! Thrift stores are hit or miss, but if you visit regularly, you'll find books for a buck or two on subjects like nature photography, quilt designs, and art history. Don't overlook the inspiration you may find in children's book illustrations. And we haven't even begun to talk about the Internet.

You can find anything online. Google "daisy art" or "ocean art" and then click on "Images" at the top of your search results. You'll get hundreds of images. Inspiration is fine. Imitate a color scheme. Study ways to draw a figure. But if you intend to use an image explicitly, be sure to ask permission and give attribution.

Here's a search process I recently did. I searched "sandhill cranes" and clicked on "Images" at the top of my results page. I was looking for photos to study, so that I might draw a sandhill crane. Rather, I fell in love with a photo that I wanted to adapt. So I had to ask permission. Had I simply studied crane images and then composed my own drawing which did not copy any single image, then I would not have needed to ask permission.

Visiting museums, collecting art books, studying the masters, and checking out local studios and galleries will broaden your rug-hooking horizons and inspire whole worlds of potential. The six design challenges here include taking inspiration from folk art and textile art; emulating master painters; adapting contemporary art, like painting, collage, and photography; and looking to other less likely media.

The Peace of Wild Things, *51" x 30", #6- through 8-cut on linen. Designed and hooked by Tamara Pavich, Council Bluffs, Iowa, 2013.*
PETER C. PHILLIPS

This rug was inspired by a piece of literary art, a poem by Wendell Berry, whose narrator goes to "lie down where the wood drake rests in his beauty on the water, and the great heron feeds." This is a poem I have memorized and recite to myself when I feel worried. I designed it in a workshop with the help of my friend and teacher, Pris Buttler. It hangs opposite my bed, so that I can see it before sleep and remember the comfort of that poem.

Lascaux Cave Horse, 34" x 25", hand-cut with scissors at approximately #6- to 8-cut wool on linen. Designed and hooked by Janet Conner, Hiram, Maine, 2014.

"The cave horse rug was made immediately after I had finished with a Gauguin adaptation," Janet said. "My creative pendulum had swung toward the highly saturated, intense colors of girls on the beach, and then back to the dark, rocky, earth tones of the cave walls of Lascaux. Looking back, I realize that it is not an accident that I gravitated to neutral colors, lots of textures, and as-is wool after the previous month's foray into dyeing sunlit colors.

"I love all art history, but the prehistoric work is one of my favorite genres. So mysterious! In caves separated by thousands of miles and thousands of years, the drawing style looks pretty consistent. I wonder why cave painters always showed beasts with small heads, dainty feet, and massive, heavy bodies. Wish I could learn more."

Home Sweet Home, 34" x 20", #2- through 4-cut wool on Scottish burlap. Adapted from a 1930s advertising booklet. Designed and hooked by Joanne Thomason, Newton, Iowa, 2015. This beautiful rug shows that art inspiration can come from anywhere. While looking at antiques in a shop, Joanne came across a small booklet advertising house paint. She suspects that the booklet dates back to the 1930s.

Start with Art 77

Design Idea #1: The Enduring Appeal of Folk Art

Art happens—no home is safe from it.
—James Abbott McNeill Whistler

Before I ever began rug hooking, I spent many hours looking at hooked rugs online. At the website of Maine fiber artist and teacher Janet Conner, I found a disarmingly simple original design. In *Shorebirds* Janet mimicked the folk art of carved bird decoys, depicting five shorebird species carved by five different folk artists. She didn't attempt to hook the realistic birds themselves, mind you, but the stick-up carved decoys created by New England carvers. A many-colored hit-or-miss border framed the simple motifs. Janet graciously hooked the rug for me, and nine years later, it still hangs in our entryway.

To design a rug inspired by folk art, let's begin with a definition. Generally, folk art is the art of self-taught people who are not trained artistically in any formal way. Imagine the retired fisherman who collected driftwood for his carvings of fish, whales, and seabirds. Or think of the prairie homemaker creating cornhusk dolls for her little girl. Like early rug-hookers, folk artists often used handy and inexpensive materials for their creations. The quilts, weather vanes, and painted furniture of the last two centuries were made for utilitarian reasons while also decorating a humble home in an affordable way. Often folk art paintings or carvings are called "naïve," in that they don't consider the traditional rules of proportion or perspective. But far from looking down on the unaffected aesthetics of folk art, many modern artists of the twentieth century studied its qualities and drew inspiration from it, just as we do today.

Many primitive rug designs have been inspired by various types of folk art. Here is an incomplete list of potential inspiration pieces:

- Quilts, coverlets, and other types of handiwork and textile art
- Stencils and wall murals
- Weather vanes and metalwork
- Paintings
- Carvings and sculptures
- Handmade dolls and toys
- Pottery
- Kitchenware, like painted pantry poxes or carved wooden bowls
- Painted furniture
- Primitive hooked rugs
- Any lovely piece of art created by a self-taught artist

To design and hook your folk-art inspired rug, there are many resources to help you, including online images from the U.S. and other cultures, beautiful books filled with photos, and even museums devoted to the preservation of folk art. Collectors of antique folk art are drawn to the weathered patina of their charming finds, and often rugs that mimic folk art are hooked in muted colors to evoke the age of the inspiration piece. Remember that we need not restrict ourselves to antiques, as there are many kinds of folk art being made today.

Shorebirds, *32" x 17½". #6 to 8-cut wool on linen. Designed and hooked by Janet Conner, Hiram, Main, 2008.* PETER C. PHILLIPS

This rug does not attempt to depict realistic shorebirds, but rather it pays tribute to folk artists, the New England carvers who created "stick-up" decoys. The hit-or-miss border enlivens the quiet composition, and shells in the corners carry out the theme of the seashore. From the collection of Tamara Pavich.

African Jumble, *36" x 36", #4-, 6-, and 8-cut wool on linen. Designed and hooked by Beth Zerweck-Tembo, Bridgewater, Virginia, 2008.*

"Walking into an African village, the first things a visitor may see are colorfully painted or sculpted walls on the outside of huts," Beth said. "These amazing examples of folk art can be found throughout the continent. Although the designs vary, African wall decoration usually displays geometric patterns, sometimes combined with abstract animals, birds, fish, or reptiles arranged in a somewhat haphazard arrangement. African Jumble is designed in this style.

"For my border, I used geometric block designs based on the mud walls of a hut in Nigeria. The animals were found on a variety of West African folk-art items: calabash containers, molded brass weights, a carved wooden door. These figures were usually highly stylized and patterned. My overall design is simple, and I was hoping for a spontaneous feel to the arrangement."

Start with Art **81**

Design Idea #2: Take Off on Textiles

Needlework arts exist in fantastic variety wherever there are women.
—Patricia Mainardi

Bleu Maison, 9½" x 14½", #4-cut wool on linen with embellishment. Designed and hooked by Val Flannigan, Kelowna, BC, 2013.

"Selecting just the right value of blue was critical for establishing definition and depth," Val said. "I chose a very pale blue grey for all the outlining. Beads were randomly placed throughout, on the top of the surface."

As rug hookers, we naturally admire the handiwork of makers from our own cultures and other cultures, a statement that is borne out in the number of textile-inspired rugs being hooked today: rugs that look like quilts, rugs that mimic batik, paisley mats, tapestry adaptations, and many textile designs taken from other cultures—African, Panamanian, and Native American, to name a few. Among the oldest rugs in this country, we can find examples that mimic intricate crewel embroidery and simple quilt patterns. Books featuring antique hooked rugs show designs hooked with jewel-toned colors and dark wool to give the look of crazy quilts made entirely of silk and velvet.

If you haven't yet looked to your favorite textiles for inspiration, maybe it's time. Back in the 1990s, Anita White was an antique dealer who first found inspiration in vintage paisley garments

82   Designed By You

and shawls. Although many paisley rug-hooking patterns of the past are designed for narrow cuts, Anita has created them for wider cuts as well. Her latest design is included here, based on a hand-embroidered piece of paisley she found in an antiques shop. If you end up hooking a paisley fabric into the design, Anita offers this advice: Choose your paisley first, and then analyze and pull colors from the paisley for the rest of the design. And cut your paisley as wide as possible to maximize its effect.

Anita is not alone in her desire to continue reinventing a beloved textile through rug-hooking designs. Barbara Carroll re-creates old coverlet patterns. Norma Batastini designs mola-inspired rugs. And Beth Tembo studies African textiles and appreciates their geometric and abstract designs. On page 57, we have included Beth's piece that mimics Kuba cut-pile embroidery weaving. Beth will continue to mine this rich vein of creativity. Her future holds more African-textile inspired rug designs based on kente weavings, adinkra prints, and bogolanfini mud cloth.

Sometimes, textile design is a one-time inspiration. For an ATHA challenge, Val Flannigan was asked to hook "a house rug of any design and size." Using a Latvian batik fabric for inspiration, she designed and hooked *Bleu Maison*.

Where will your textile inspiration come from? My next project is a pair of ottomans that look as though they are upholstered with mud cloth. My friends have hooked large rugs and runners similar to Native American weaving. Do you relish the texture in wedding blankets of Morocco? Do the dazzling colors of Peruvian rugs speak to you? Would you like to hook your own Turkish kilim? Cut a piece of linen and pick up your marker. So many textiles. So little time.

Kashmir Runner, *49" x 19", #8-cut wool and #8.5-cut paisley on linen. Designed and hooked by Anita White, Overland Park, Kansas, 2016.*

This rug was based on a beautiful piece of paisley that Anita found in a St. Louis antique shop. "It is entirely hand embroidered, and the color is remarkably vibrant," she said. "I hooked this paisley rug in December and January while dealing with lumbar pain. It was my therapy!"

Start with Art 83

Design Idea #3: Hooking to Abstraction

There is no abstract art. You must always start with something. Afterward you can remove all traces of reality.

—Pablo Picasso

The term "abstract art" sounds awfully lofty and sophisticated and, well, hoity-toity. A rug hooker may worry that she can't understand the concept, let alone make her own piece of abstract art. Yet what is abstract art if not a liberation from rules? As Wanda Kerr has demonstrated, we can approach it by doodling shapes and squiggles and stick figures. Children joyfully and playfully make abstract art until they grow up and become afraid of it.

So let's not be afraid of it. Let's describe abstract art and give it a try in our own designs. Usually its shapes, patterns, lines, colors, and textures are what make it interesting. Rather than making a realistic picture of something, abstract artists wish to achieve an effect or evoke a response. Viewers of abstract art play an important role; they get to interpret the abstract image.

Some abstract paintings include recognizable, realistic elements. For instance, Roslyn Logsdon's *Three of Us* is realistic in its human figures, but the abstraction is accomplished through the surprising use of color. There is a lesser degree of abstraction in *Three of Us* than in *Joy*, which uses the same color palette. Here, Roslyn made no marks on the linen. She hooked one shape, and "the rest of the design flowed from it," she said. *Joy* includes no realistic or identifiable motifs.

Here are several design ideas to use as springboards into an abstract rug. Remember that these categories are not mutually exclusive.

Repeating patterns please the eye, so look for an object or shape to use in creating a repeating pattern design. Consider patterns of circles, squares, or arches, or use everyday objects like spoons or rakes. Take an image from nature like a bed of ferns or a flock of birds and create your repeating pattern.

Three of Us, *14" x 36", #3- and 4-cut wool on burlap. Designed and hooked by Roslyn Logsdon, Laurel, Maryland, 1973.*

Roslyn's Three of Us *is a portrait that has been divided into many separate fields of color. This method of abstraction requires a keen sense of color and value.* "I was interested in capturing the essence of the figures while simplifying the shapes," Roslyn said. "My teacher in graduate school stressed simplicity, and it became my mantra. I found that limiting the color range could result in exciting variations. Three of Us includes myself holding my son David upside down. Michael is the glow in my body." *During this period in the '70s, Roslyn used the same color scheme--reds, oranges, and pinks—for a number of what she calls "semi-abstract" designs depicting family and friends.* "I still return to those colors," *she said.*

Joy, *12 ½" x 16 ½", #3- and 4-cut on linen. Designed and hooked by Roslyn Logsdon, Laurel, Maryland, 1975.*
  Roslyn did not draw a design on the linen, but just began hooking this abstract rug. "The color flowed and moved back and forth on the two-dimensional surface," she said. "I named the piece Joy *because of the lines of color that seemed to dance across the surface of the rug."*

Fields of color abstracts a realistic image by identifying the light-, medium-, and dark-valued areas and assigning wool values and colors to those areas. See *Three of Us* by Roslyn Logsdon.

Adapt an abstract painting, always beginning by contacting the artist to ask permission.

The doodle approach takes the mystery and intimidation out of a concept like abstract art. Wanda Kerr honors the art of doodling at her online classroom, *The Welcome Mat.*

Pattern-free hooking means that you cut a piece of linen and leave it blank with no markings to guide you. Begin to pull loops and see what appears under your hook.

  Whatever jumping-off point you choose, whatever method works best, make the leap away from realism and try hooking an abstract.

Start with Art **85**

Design Idea #4: Adapting Someone Else's Art

When you are captivated by something, you think "Could I do that? Hmm, let me try."

—Curtis Sittenfeld

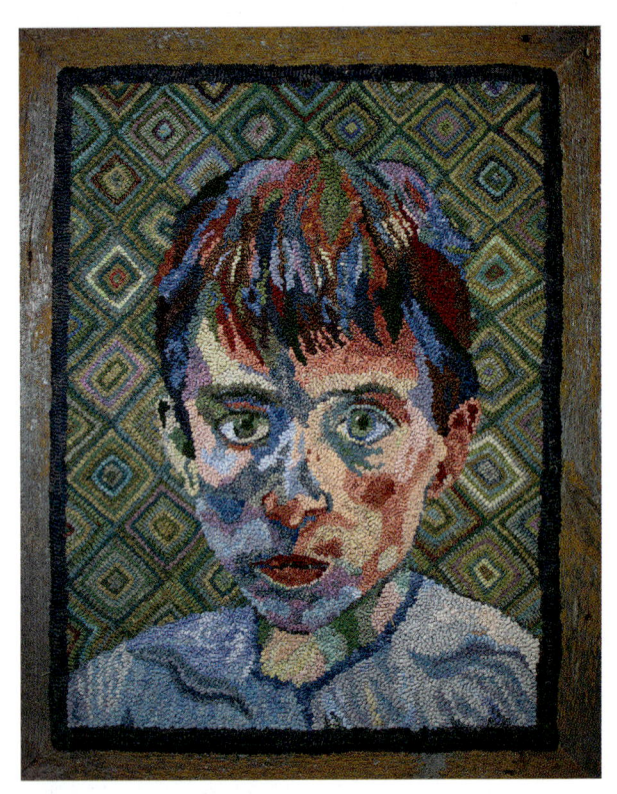

Baseball Diamond, *23" x 30", #4- through 6-cut wool on linen. Adapted with permission from a pencil drawing by David Phillips. Designed and hooked by Tamara Pavich, Council Bluffs, Iowa, 2016.* PETER C. PHILLIPS

Some years ago, my brother Dave did realistic pencil sketches of our nieces and nephew, and he gave me permission to enlarge the sketches and hook them. I wanted to play with color in the faces. Donna Hrkman was my teacher, and she helped me render the faces, mostly with #5-cut. Christian, my nephew loves baseball, so the background of this rug is green baseball diamonds. He's a very talented young man, so he's really the baseball "diamond" here.

BOTTOM LEFT: Isabella Arabesque, *23" x 30", #4- through 6-cut wool on linen. Adapted with permission from a pencil drawing by David Phillips. Designed and hooked by Tamara Pavich, Council Bluffs, Iowa, 2016.* PETER C. PHILLIPS

Even though my background shapes are wonky, the arabesque is a graceful and lovely shape, like Isabella herself. Her colors are overwhelmingly cool, but I'm glad for the warm shades that temper it a little.

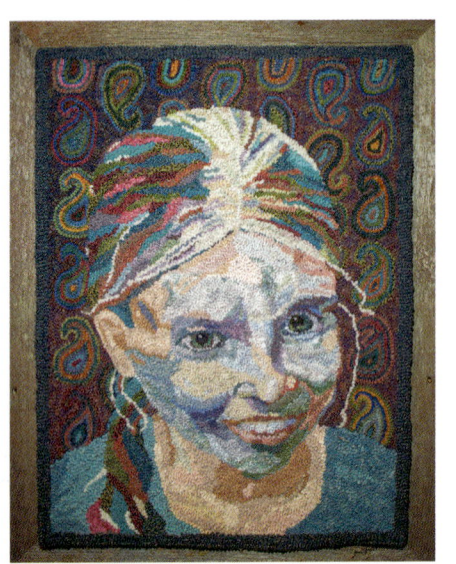

LEFT: Gracie in Paisley, *23" x 30", #4- through 6-cut wool on linen. Adapted with permission from a pencil drawing by David Phillips. Designed and hooked by Tamara Pavich, Council Bluffs, Iowa, 2016.* PETER C. PHILLIPS

For this last portrait of the three, I wanted a lively background Anita White (the queen of paisley) helped me find just the right paisley pattern. Again, it is wonky—it has an element of fun that matches Gracie's sweet smile.

You're window shopping in a hip part of town, and suddenly your heart stops. You are smitten with a piece of art. But it's not yours to adapt yet. In this instance, we all know what to do. We make an inquiry, obtain the artist's permission, and then see what we can make in our medium of wool.

If you haven't been smitten yet, then an exploration is in order. Artists immerse themselves in the study of art, and there are many ways to do it. Perhaps the most refreshing suggestion we can make is to invite a friend to accompany you to the galleries and museums in your area.

Tower of Fish, *18" x 24", #9-cut wool on linen. Adapted with permission from the painting by Charles Houska. Designed and hooked by Nola Heidbreder, St. Louis, Missouri, 2015.*

"Charlie gave us permission to use six of his designs to hook for a challenge," Nola said. "After the pieces were hooked, he graciously let us have a show of the hooked pieces in his gallery in February 2015. We were all attracted to the bright colors, the wide lines (perfect for a #9 cut), the animals, and the whimsical designs."

It is remarkable how much ground we can cover with online searches, and if you don't know where to begin, searching Google by subject matter will get you started. Enter search terms "oak branches art," for instance, and on your results page, click on "Images" at the very top of your screen. My search resulted in thousands of images: botanical prints of various oak species; paintings, drawings, and photographs of oak trees from all perspectives; and clip art, which is often in the public domain.

An essential first step in the process of adapting contemporary art is contacting the original artist and asking permission. If we adapt without permission, we risk both our finances and our reputation. Please see pages 78 for more on the subject of copyright and adaptation.

Here are a few observations about the artists I have met when asking permission to adapt their art:
- Artists I have met take a kind and generous attitude toward other artists, and they are usually curious about an unusual textile art like wool rug hooking.
- Artists I have met are both grateful for the courtesy and honored by the compliment of being asked about adaptation. Some, however, have been burned by people who used their images without asking permission. They may need assurance that only a single rug will be made, and that the rug will not be sold.
- Artists I have met would like to see examples of hooked rugs. If they give permission for adaptation, they want a photo of the resulting wool rug and may publish the adaptation themselves, often online.
- Artists that my fellow rug hookers and I have approached for permission to hook adaptations respond with warmth and sometimes with lasting friendship.

When your art exploration turns up a captivating image, reach out to the artist with your request. If the answer is no, don't lose heart. You will find another image to adapt and an artist who will gladly guide you along the road to originality.

Design Idea #5: More and More Media

Good painting is the kind that looks like sculpture.

—Michelangelo

Garden Buddha, 14" x 14", #3-, 4-, and 6-cut wool on linen. Designed and hooked by Lou Ann Ayres, Papillion, Nebraska, 2015.

"For years, I gardened around this Buddha sculpture and made special places for him in my garden," Lou Ann said. "I drew my pattern from a picture I took of the statue. On this rug, I needed to create the pitting seen in my photograph that was the result of being out in my yard for 20 years. To see the natural highlights and moss were essential in making a somewhat monochromatic figure come to life. I wanted to see the imperfections that were created by elements while not losing the vision and serenity of the subject matter."

Lou Ann's rug was recognized by the Bellevue Art Association of Bellevue, Nebraska, and won artist of the month in October 2015. "Having others see rug hooking as art is a great accomplishment," she said.

That quote from Michelangelo may not seem relevant to rug hooking. Yet many rug hookers are using three-dimensional art to inspire them. My third article for *Rug Hooking* magazine reported on a Nova Scotia art show, "Hooked on Swoon," that invited rug hookers to adapt art pieces of various media. Twenty-two adaptations resulted, with inspiration coming from all kinds of art. Besides the oils and watercolors, rug hookers selected pottery, stained glass, and folk-art carvings to inspire them.

I continually come across rug hookers who recognize no boundaries for their inspiration. They have hooked ancient cave art and mosaics. They have adapted wood-cuts and tapestries. They have gone beyond two-dimensional art to pottery and sculpture. The world of art is deep and wide, this design

The Pomegranate Tree,
22" x 28", #7- and 8-cut wool on linen. Designed and hooked by Anne Marie Lewis, Omaha, Nebraska, 2014.

Anne Marie has studied ancient mosaics and their meanings. This is an adaptation of a floor mosaic from the Caesarea Church in Israel. It was created in the sixth century, and the artist is unknown. According to Anne Marie's research, the pomegranate was a symbol of learning, wisdom, and fertility. "My light and medium purple shades fill in for worn away or separated tiles," Anne Marie said, "where the mortar shows under and between the mosaic tiles. The other tones honor the simplicity of the original mosaic; they provide contrast with the purples and the golds in the ripening fruit."

Anne Marie is concerned that these priceless, ancient works of art are being lost, and says "My mission is to hook more ancient mosaics, to preserve these images."

idea offers encouragement to broaden our exploration into more and more media.

Lou Ann Ayres took a photo of a dear garden sculpture she had owned for 20 years, so in one way, Lou Ann was adapting a two-dimensional photograph. But it was very important to her to make this rug look like the sculpture in three dimensions. Her rug incorporates the relief of the facial features, and it mimics moss and the pitting that resulted from decades of exposure to the elements. The piece won a local art award, earning recognition from other artists.

For Anne Marie Lewis, "every hooked rug is a mosaic image," because the loops cast shadows that look like the grout between the mosaic pieces. Anne Marie is fascinated with ancient mosaics, particularly those in Israel, and she has made quite a study of them. Hooking them is satisfying, especially because the medium of hooking loops creates the look of a mosaic in stone. While the ancient mosaic floors are deteriorating, adapting these images is one way of preserving them, Anne Marie says.

Janet Conner places no limits on the types of art she will adapt or use for inspiration. Her list is long, including "tribal art, anthropological artifacts, African masks, Celtic and Mayan symbols, cave art, tapa cloth, Egyptian art, and the ancient Bayeaux tapestry."

You'll find a wealth of new ideas if you cast your net wider, across all artistic media, two- or three-dimensional. Get thee to a gallery and find inspiration. Or it may be as near as your own garden.

Start with Art 89

Design Idea #6: Learning from the Masters

The most an artist can do is say, let me show you what I have seen, what I have loved, and perhaps you will see it and love it too.

—Annie Bevan

As we become students of fine art and of master artists, we will almost certainly become enamored of certain works. Eventually we narrow our focus to the one work we want to study and adapt.

In her 1969 book, *Rug Hooking and Rag Tapestries*, Ann Wiseman encouraged her readers to "adapt from the masters." She herself hooked an adaptation of Picasso's magnificent *Guernica*, believing that "art is derived from art," that "no apology need be made for adaptation or influence. It is a means to understanding, but out if it must grow originality."

If you feel the least pang of guilt about "copying" an artist, remember this: Most artists began as apprentices or practiced imitation during their fledgling years. In his youth, Michelangelo apprenticed with several sculptors and painters. American painter Andrew Wyeth sat at his father's knee, learning the art of illustration before developing his own style and subject matter. Very late in his career, Vincent Van Gogh studied and imitated the paintings of Jean-François Millet. Usually the titles of these works are followed by the words "after Millet," and today, these paintings are among the most valuable works of Van Gogh.

Many teachers of rug hooking include fine art adaptation in their offerings. Janet Conner has distinguished herself as a teacher of Van Gogh adaptations (among other artists). "Fine-art principles are always important for rug hookers," Janet said, "and a teacher can illustrate art principles through teaching fine-art adaptation." Cathy Stephan uses wide cuts when teaching the works of Jean-François Millet. "One is not able to reproduce each brushstroke," Cathy said, "therefore, you must simplify the master's work in your rendition. Seeing values that are close and then improvising with wool is a big challenge." For many years, Pris Buttler has been using the works of Gustav Klimt in her teaching, and more recently she has introduced the works of Claude Monet, Georgia O'Keeffe, and Dutch master Jan Theodore Toorop. Pris encourages emulation more often than explicit adaptation of specific masterworks. When they emulate a master painter, "students can see how it feels to follow in another's footsteps," she said, "with at least part of the plan already worked out for them."

By all means, sign up for workshops with teachers who use fine art adaptation in their rug-hooking instruction. Or begin your apprenticeship on your own. Google your favorite master painter and click on "Images." Pick up an art book and spend the evening studying the paintings. Look back at Chapter 2 for ways to draw a favorite fine art design. When you're ready, cut a piece of linen and draw. Hooking a fine art adaptation will carry you one step closer to developing your own style and your own body of work.

The Gleaners, *52" x 40", #6- through #8.5-cut wool on linen. Designed and hooked by Cathy Stephan, Athens, Wisconsin, 2014.*

"I always had this adaption of the masterful painting by Jean-Françoise Millet on my bucket list," Cathy said, "and finally finished it in 2014. There have been many prints made of The Gleaners, and I chose one from a library book, with brighter more beautiful colors.

"I was amazed at the variety of colors Millet used in any one skirt or shirt, and I could not use each color I saw, because my 'brushstrokes' were so much wider than the painter's strokes. I simplified. For instance, for the skirt worn by the woman on the right, I skipped around to indigo, plum, black, and even a bit of purple, which were the colors I saw in the painting. That was a lot of fun and kept my interest.

"'Painting the light' with woolens was fun, too. I jazzed up the top of the scarves that would have been in the sunshine, and toned way down for the shadows. Thankfully my stash is large, and I didn't have to do much dyeing. I ended up using wools that were mistakes from the dye pot and had been sitting on my shelves for years. My dye-pot failures ended up working beautifully in the some of the ground areas."

Start with Art 91

(Learning from the Masters continued)

92   Designed By You

Couple in Garden with Blue Fir Tree, 22" x 28", various cuts of wool, up to #8-cut (much of it hand-cut) on linen. Adapted from the 1888 Van Gogh painting of the same name. Designed and hooked by Norma Brimstein, Rochester, New York, 2015.

"I've seen several printed editions of this painting, ranging from very bright to quite subdued. I began to hook it bright, but the road looked too flat and the blue fir tree was becoming too green. So, as I often do—ignoring the advice of every teacher I've ever had—I ripped it all out and started over. Immediately, with the addition of the grays in contrast with the ivory, the road began to 'solidify' and come alive with light and shadow under the couple's feet.

"I've come to the conclusion that in order to achieve the look of a Van Gogh, you've got to replicate his brush strokes with your hooking, and that seems to happen only when you use a multitude of shades, hooked next to one another, avoiding placing two like strips side-by-side as much as possible."

For more about Norma's Van Gogh rug hooking see her Courage-to-Draw story in Chapter 2.

OPPOSITE, TOP: Starry Night, 24" x 36", scissor-cut wool at about #7-cut on linen. Adapted from the Van Gogh painting of the same name. Designed by Janet Conner, and hooked by her daughter, Rachael T. Conner, Hiram, Maine, 2007.

Rachael used hand-dyed, recycled woolens to mimic the brushstrokes of Van Gogh, adapting what is perhaps his most famous painting today, an isolated village nestled in the hills of the French countryside, with the dynamic night sky above.

"This was Rachael's very first rug," Janet said, "and she worked on and off for over a year to complete it. In 2010, Rachael's Starry Night was shown at the Farnsworth Museum's show entitled "Beyond Rugs," curated by author and rug collector Mildred Peladeau.

OPPOSITE, BOTTOM: Tahitian Women on the Beach, 42" x 30", wool hand-cut at about #6 or 7, on primitive unbleached linen. Adapted from the painting by Paul Gauguin. Designed and hooked by Janet Conner, Hiram, Maine, 2014.

"After adapting several Van Gogh paintings, Janet turned to his close friend and fellow post-impressionist Paul Gauguin for inspiration. "I was attracted to this painting as much for the dyeing as the hooking," Janet said. Janet knew she would need at least four gradated shades of each color to "show dimensionality through values."

Having come to rug hooking from a career as an art teacher, Janet helps her rug-hooking students do close and detailed analysis of a work of art in order to raise their visual awareness and appreciation for the artist. Hooking a piece that is inspired by fine art, she says, "brings a satisfying sense of accomplishment, and a great rug that will never go out of style. Most of all, we learn to create a rug which is not a copy, but a personal interpretation, inspired by our chosen artist."

Start with Art

6

Start with Materials

Do what you can with what you have.
—Theodore Roosevelt

Sometimes, a rug-hooker seeking design inspiration need look no further than her own stash. We surely know that our wool can get our creative juices flowing, but we're not used to looking to our shelves for design inspiration. Though we can easily imagine rugs inspired by art or color, style or story, it's far less common to consider that our rug-making materials could actually prompt a design.

But it happens more often than we think. As I mentioned in the early pages of this book, my friends and I used to play a little game as we hooked together. Someone would find an interesting piece of wool and drop it in the center of our table. "What would you hook with that?" one of us would say. A speckled fat quarter would be deemed perfect for hooking chicken feathers or the centers of flowers. A houndstooth could render the rough bark of a tree trunk. Tiny checks might make realistic shingles on a cottage roof. And on we went, considering all kinds of wool and what we might make of it. Without even realizing it, we were beginning to design rugs in our minds.

Hebridean Abstract, *30" x 26", #3- through 8-cut Harris Tweed yarn and wool on linen. Designed and hooked by Brigitte Webb, Dingwall, Scotland, 2013.*

"This is a story rug in abstract form," Brigitte said. "A very good friend of mine called Donella McKenzie has a cousin, Ena Campbell, in her eighties, who after seeing one of my rugs asked if I would like to have her collection of Harris tweed yarns and wool left over from clothes she had made for herself and family. This lovely lady has lived all her life on the west coast of Scotland in a place called Rhue. I felt very honored to receive the materials, and about the same time, Donella gave me her dad's favorite Harris Tweed jacket. He had been a war veteran.

"So the inspiration came for me to hook Donella and her husband a floor rug. I thought I would do it in an abstract manner that would conjure up what Harris and the West Coast means—its ruggedness, hills, heathers, rivers, rocks, sea, isolation, open spaces, tranquility. All these locally made materials are the life blood of the island. I did not use any other materials in this rug other than these, including her dad's jacket. Initially I just drew a few random meandering lines, starting in the middle. It was lovely seeing this rug evolve out of feelings and thoughts, and I know how much it means to my friend."

Ballerinas Someday, *30" x 15", yarn and tulle on rug warp. Designed and hooked by Kay LeFevre, Windsor, Ontario, 2013.*

"I wanted to capture the playfulness of tiny ballerinas," Kay said, "who one moment take it very seriously and the next treat the bar like a playground. I had the idea to use tulle as a 3-D feature and took off from there. I used a photo of my granddaughter's ballet class and added additional ballerinas. My favorite part is the reflections made in the shiny wood floor, along with the tutus."

"Rough cloth strips often bring good effects when parti-colored in stripes or with dots. This is advised for certain mosaic and wavy variegated backgrounds, flowers, etc."
—William Winthrop Kent, The Hooked Rug, *1941*

In this chapter, Start with Materials, we include design ideas for using ragged torn strips of wool rather than machine-cut strips; we suggest designs suited to textured wools so loved by author Stella Hay Rex and teacher Cathy Stephan; and we show how artists have designed around yarns and other fibers. Next we explore rugs inspired by embellishment materials; ways of using leftover noodles; and finally, creative ways of incorporating other textile arts into our hooked pieces.

Another way of being inspired by our materials is to use what I call "family fabrics" from the clothing of people we have loved. Marilyn Becker hooked an image of her father as a young man. To hook his shirt, she cut strips from his actual shirt which she had saved for decades after he passed away. Some hookers have taken the baby clothes that their children have outgrown to hook toys and animals into a memory rug. Hooking the garments of our family members—their skirts, suits, and dresses—into our designs is a way of keeping dear ones present in our lives.

Sit down in your wool room and open your mind. Look through your rovings, fleece, and other fibers. Ponder your silks and paisleys and velvets. Don't forget those spools of shimmering, glittering stuff, which could trace the paths of faeries through a forest!

Generating Design Ideas 97

Design Idea #1: Go on a Tear

Maggie Bonanomie taught us to tear strips . . .
I haven't used my cutter since.

—Theresa Rapstein Schafer

Georgia O'Keeffe, 34" x 24", torn wool strips and #8-cut wool on linen. Designed and hooked by Pris Buttler, Gainesville, Georgia, 2012.
Pris wanted to demonstrate that shading can be executed in wider cuts, so she rendered these Georgia O'Keeffe-style flowers almost entirely in torn strips.

Every once in a while, you meet a rug hooker who shatters your assumptions about hooking. Wanda Kerr was one of those people for me. I had seen rugs done in torn strips, usually primitive with a capital *P*. But I never dreamed that someone could create a detailed, realistic portrait using a #12 cut. Regardless of the width of her strips, Wanda puts no restrictions on her expectations, proving that we can render whatever we like in wool, even very wide-cut or torn strips of wool. (See her self-portrait, *Town Hooker*, on page 142.)

Here is your chance to put the cutter away and create a rug from wide, torn strips, and we begin with a few practical suggestions. You may wish to make scissor snips an inch apart along the edge of your pieces of wool for easier tearing. Some loosely woven wools will shred in the process of tearing. In these cases, Cathy Stephan encourages us to tear strips that are two inches wide and then use our scissors to cut those double-wide strips down the middle. If you're used to using smaller cuts, you'll be amazed at how quickly you can complete a torn-strips project, and here are two very different examples to tempt you.

Like Wanda, Pris Buttler wanted to demonstrate that the potential of wide-cut hooking is not so different from using narrower cuts. She created a glorious floral rug done in the style of Georgia O'Keeffe to demonstrate that fine shading can indeed be done with torn strips.

Using muted colors, Cathy Stephan achieved a more primitive look and feel with her sweet design, *Olde Maine Floral*, emphasizing the wavy edges of her torn-strip loops in the petals and leaves of her flowers.

If this is your first torn-strips design, keep it simple. You might try a primitive pictorial with a single motif, like a house, a cat, or a padula, with a hit-or-miss border. Get out your cookie cutters and choose a few simple images to enlarge for your design. Perhaps you would prefer a chunky little geometric for your hearth, like three nine-patch quilt blocks.

To alter the look of your finished piece, you can cut some or all of your loops. Wide-cut rugs with cut loops are sometimes called "Lulu rugs" after Lulu Meyers, a prolific rug hooker who routinely cut the loops of her hooked rugs, giving them a shirred look.

Finally, keep sore-muscle cream at hand in case you need it. You may notice a little strain in your hand and arm as you pull those fat and squishy loops through your linen.

Olde Maine Floral, *36" x 60", hand-torn wool strips on linen. Designed and hooked by Cathy Stephan, Athens, Wisconsin, 2015.*

"This design came from an old rug found in an attic in Maine," Cathy said. "It had a dirty greenish background, and I changed it to green/brown, black, and brown textures, which contributes to the old look.

"I love the craggy, irregular look of a torn strip rug," Cathy said. "It reminds me of the look of shirred rugs of the past. I have done several. You may not get much detail into these rugs, and you really don't want to. Torn strips give you the look of wavy edges, which I love.

"Doing torn strip rugs is a harder 'pull' for your loops, and you have to get used to the height of the loops. They must be high to get that falling-over, squished look when they are walked on. That is all part of the learning fun with reproducing antique rugs."

Start with Materials **99**

Design Idea #2: Maximum Texture

*If I could preach from the housetops,
I would reiterate mixtures, mixtures, and more mixtures—
tweeds, plaids, checks, mottled goods of all description.*

—Stella Hay Rex

The Day My Dad Came Home From the War, 14¼" x 18¼", #3-cut wool on linen. Adapted from a family photograph. Designed and hooked by Connie Lorch, London, Ontario, 2013.

"The photo was taken by my grandparents," Connie said, "and my parents had it on a table in the living room with my dad's hat hanging over the corner of it. I can remember looking at it every time I went into the living room. Almost the moment I saw someone hooking in black, white, and grays, I knew I wanted to hook the picture of Dad and Mom when he came home from the war.

"People often comment on the wool I used for my mother's coat and how much it looks exactly like her coat in the photo. I knew the look I wanted to capture even though I had never actually seen my mother's coat or my dad's uniform. My mother was a rug hooker, and I keep thinking how very proud she would be."

"I have nothing against solid woolens," Cathy Stephan said. "But the ones with lots of little speckles of colors fascinate me to work with and to look at once I am done." These textured wools, in fact, inspired Cathy's *Rose Star Runner*, in which she created eight-point stars on which to bestow every texture in her stash. Having been smitten with Cathy's use of textured wools myself, I hooked my own version of the *Rose Star Runner* in a workshop. Cathy patiently explained how she achieved her desired effect by placing textured row within textured row until each star almost twinkles with those "pixels of color" in the wools.

This design idea asks you to make yourself a nice pile of textured wools and ruminate on them. What future rug is in that pretty pile? Is there a chunky pillow for a cozy corner? Would a repeating shape or pattern—like Cathy's eight-pointed stars—show off the beautiful textures in your stash? A pair of mittens, a scattering of oak leaves, a border of lamb's tongues: what will please you most in showing off your delicious woolens?

If you're short on textures, start looking for them. We all have our favorites. Some hookers maintain that recycled woolens—the wools from disassembled coats, suits, and other garments—produce the yummiest results when hooked. These hookers scour sales and thrift shops for such treasures. Others collect herringbones, those angled parallel lines like the bones of a fish. An oversized herringbone pattern or the tiny delicate ones never fail to satisfy when hooked into a rug. And ah, the delights of bouclé, that wool with two textures, rough on the front and smooth on the back. Long ago, my first-ever rug was the simple figure of an owl perched inside a half moon against a deep blue sky. For the owl, my teacher suggested a gray/brown bouclé. Hooking the owl with this wool was deeply rewarding, as the little fellow looked like he had actual feathers, due to those two textures hooked into the motif. That bouclé had a lot to do with my falling in love with rug hooking.

Your design need not be primitive in order to be inspired by a textured wool. Connie Lorch found just the perfect material to hook her mother's coat in the realistic photograph adaptation shown here. Many sepia photograph adaptations have benefited greatly from heavily textured tan and brown wools that do much of the work of creating a realistic image.

So gather your stripes, your plaids and tweeds, those precious recycled woolens, and ask yourself--what does this wool want to be? Whatever design you create, enjoy the rich, textured results.

BELOW: Rose Star Runner, *29" x 89" (for the version that is seven blocks in length), #8- and 8.5-cut wool on linen. Designed and hooked by Cathy Stephan, Athens, Wisconsin, 2012.* PETER C. PHILLIPS

Cathy started this rug while she was laid up with a six-week illness. "I wanted to profile special wools that would add interest and movement as the eye travels over the piece," she said. "Tweeds, herringbone, and honeycomb wools in many colors provided the interest with their pixels of colors." While Cathy loves all woolens, she often selects those that stimulate visually with speckles or pixels of color.

"I started out with an 8.5 cut, but decided I wanted more rows of color and more detail in each star, so I went down to the #8 cut. I did each of the backgrounds in different darks to prove that it is about value more than about color."

Note: Because of photography challenges, this *Rose Star Runner* was actually hooked by Tamara Pavich, but the goal was to imitate Cathy's runner as explicitly as possible.

Start with Materials 101

Design Idea #3: Fiber: More Is More

Every fiber of my being tells me to hook with every fiber in my stash!
—Anonymous

"**Lately I have been hooking only with yarn** to use up my ever-growing stash," Sharon Johnston said. "The beauty of yarn is the wonderful supply of colors, thickness, and textures that can be used in so many ways. Yarn doesn't require cutting into strips, which is a big time saver.... The loops can be pulled high or low, twisted or sculpted."

Sharon's rugs hooked entirely with yarn have been published in Judy Taylor's book, *Rug Hooker's Guide to the Yarniverse!* (Judy has written several books on the subject.) While hooking entirely with yarn is one option, many traditional rug hookers begin hooking with cut strips of wool and eventually become inspired to add other kinds of fiber to their projects. This design idea is about filling your mind with beautiful fibers and conjuring the perfect design for them. Be warned—once you open up to yarns and fibers, you could become a collector.

Several years ago, a group of Nebraska hookers visited a Jacob's sheep farm, whose owners produce knobbly textured yarns. At that time, the visitors weren't hooking with yarn, but were buying lots of it for binding and finishing rugs. They enjoyed learning about this ancient breed from England and its springy fleece, sought after by weavers, and they nearly filled their car with fiber loot from the farm. Since then, they have seen the hooking potential in Jacob's wool yarn and pulled many loops in black, white, cream, and gray.

Rug-hooking artist and teacher Deanne Fitzpatrick of Amhurst, Nova Scotia, has created a DVD about hooking, in which she demonstrates the use of yarns and other fibers. Deanne's beautiful designs and fiber choices were so inspiring to our group that we devoted an entire weekend to imitating her and especially to incorporating a variety of fibers into our rugs: sari silk, dyed seam binding, fleeces and rovings, cut velvet, yarn, and string. Right about then, we met an alpaca farmer who sells raw fibers and yarns, both natural and dyed, to rug hookers. We began attending the fairs of spinners and weavers in our area. And, of course, we frequent our local yarn shops, always on the lookout for appealing textures and colors for our rugs. At our annual hook-in, we invited yarn vendors of all kinds: slubby ones, fuzzy ones, and even fibers that glitter and sparkle. Diane Cox, of Cornwall, uses cottons, knits, t-shirts, and felted wool in her hookings. A complete list of fibers with hooking potential probably doesn't exist, but let's all keep adding to it.

Take a look at these examples of original rug designs in which yarns play either a leading role or a supporting one. Go on a fiber hunt of your own. And then consider designing a new rug around your favorite.

**OPPOSITE PAGE:
Isabelle's Whale,**
35" x 59", #9-cut wool and wool yarn on linen. Designed and hooked by Holly McMillan, Roca, Nebraska, 2014.

"I actually started with a cool piece of roving," Holly said. "I had color-planned the rug around that roving and the colors of our bathroom. I had decided on tile for the kids' bathroom, and it is very cold. So this rug was drawn to fit most of the floor space in front of the double sinks. It has been in use for one year, and thank God no toothpaste has gotten on it.

"The roving was a beautiful blue/green piece perfect for the water, so I decided a fuchsia/pink whale was perfect for the space. The reality was that the roving was never going to be able to hold up to the traffic and abuse a floor rug gets. I ordered three different wool yarns to compare, and one matched that roving perfectly, but a word of advice. It is a bear to get the roving out after it is put in. That was a project by itself. Here's my little pearl: I usually block my rugs and then hook in the yarn afterwards. That way it stays more 3-D."

Zebra Back, *9" x 13", yarn on rug warp. Designed and hooked by Kay LeFevre, Windsor, Ontario, 2012.*

Kay's rugs, hooked entirely with yarn, have been featured in the books of Judy Taylor and in Rug Hooking magazine. "I wanted to make the mane and tail of the zebra three-dimensional," Kay said. "To draw my pattern, I used two photos of zebras, one for a face I liked and another for the behind. This was the smallest mat I had ever made, and I found it to be hard to get the detail I wanted. I was really pleased, though, with the way the 3-D parts turned out. Even the eyelashes are 3-D."

Start with Materials 103

Design Idea #3: Rug Bling

I try not to let sanity get in the way of my accessorizing.
—bumper sticker

While we all take great satisfaction from a finished wool rug, some designs simply beg for that something extra. We're calling it "rug bling," but the more common term is "embellishment." Never has rug embellishment been more popular, and in fact, today a rug hooker can take workshops on the topic, exploring many lovely materials that can enhance our rug designs.

When I think of embellishing rugs, two words come to mind: relevant and meaningful. Although embellishment for its own sake is great fun, there's something even more special about cases when the embellishment is somehow relevant to the design and adds meaning to it. A great example is the multitude of miniature steampunk embellishments that Donna Hrkman suggests adding to a steampunk rug design. Perhaps because of the contrast between soft wool and hard metal, objects like gears, watch parts, antique keys, metal brads, and Victorian jewelry complement steampunk designs in an especially pleasing and meaningful way.

One of my favorite examples of meaningful rug embellishment was actually done on a commercial pattern. My friend, Denise Hoffman, who comes from a Nebraska ranching family, hooked a charming design of five cowboy boots, and then embellished the rug with antique silver conches and loops of rope, sewn with fishing line onto the backing. Her coils of rope were nestled between rows of hooking. The finished product made a beautiful symbol of Denise's family, who have worked their cattle ranch for generations.

My imagination will not be sufficient to make a comprehensive list of embellishment possibilities. Here are a few to get our imaginative juices working. Beads of all kinds can be readily sewn on the surface of a rug (see *Bleu Maison*, by Val Flannigan on page 82). Glittering pieces of costume jewelry can dress up a portrait or adorn a Christmas tree. Bunches of raffia can make your scarecrow jump right off the rug. Buttons, antique or new, add beautiful bling. I have begun collecting antique wire-rimmed eyeglasses, with a mind toward hooking myopic characters in the future. Wooden stuff, metal stuff, ceramic stuff: once you begin thinking about embellishment, little rug-bling things start showing up everywhere.

Remembrance, 51½" x 20", hand-dyed wool yarn, sari-silk ribbon, and clay embellishments on rug warp. Designed and hooked by Karen D. Miller, Ottawa, Ontario, Canada, 2015.

Karen has almost always incorporated other materials into her hooking, but Remembrance was unusual in that this piece actually began with the creation of those 11 leaves of clay. She composed the design around them. Karen sewed strips of silk sari ribbon to the backing in order to provide a texture akin to tree bark.

"Autumn is a time of contradictions," Karen said, "of the fiery oranges and deep reds of the changing leaves, and the cool days and cold nights. As winter arrives, the leaves have fallen and only a few stragglers, dry and brown, still cling to the branches and rattle in the breeze, reminding us of what is gone. Remembrance uses the symbolism of seasonal change to explore the concept of memory. Just as a tree sheds its leaves, so too do we lose our memories with the passage of time. Those memories that are retained undergo a change in their shape and texture, just like those leaves that hang on to the branches until the very end. Stretching the design over three panels enhances the viewer's interaction with the story."

Shell Purse, 7" x 11" (7" x 5" folded), various materials on linen. Designed and hooked by Val Flannigan, Kelowna, British Columbia, 2009.

"This whole design was based on materials provided in a workshop with Michele Micarelli," Val said. "The class was given a blank piece of linen and a bag of mixed fibers: assorted silks, wired ribbon, cotton, batiks, pantyhose, velour, lace, wool, ribbons. We also found shells, beads, and assorted alternative fabrics. We were to hook a seaside bag, and the idea was to use the turn-over flap as our shoreline. I used the green silks and ribbon to create seaweed. The shells help create the shoreline and the beads give the effect of bubbles in the water."

Start with Materials 105

Design Idea #5: Nothing But Noodles

Waste not, want not.
—Ben Franklin

After hooking even half a dozen rugs, every hooker soon learns that the noodles begin to pile up. Try as we might to cut only what we need, we end up with extra worms, as Brigitte Webb calls them. While these colorful strips were the cat's meow when our rug was in progress, they somehow become a surplus commodity once the rug is done. I have plastic bags of them in drawers, and others in totes. I have tried to color-coordinate my noodles for easier use, but most of them are still there in their groups of greens, reds, and browns, taking up precious space.

Excess noodles are such a common problem that using them up is a popular group challenge. Members are required to hook a rug using only wool that has been cut, often dipping into each other's stashes for a few bits of needed color. My friend Judy Roth organizes "noodle nights" for her hookers, where everyone makes some attempt to hook cut wool into their rugs. To carry out the theme, she serves pasta noodles for supper. For our annual hook-in, the decorating committee decided to make centerpieces out of Mason jars full of colorful noodles. We were all clamoring to give them away.

Well, at some point we have the eureka moment: suppose we actually designed rugs around our noodles? That was the idea behind the *Amazing Matrix* rugs of Jennifer Manuell, of Ontario. Jen has created beautiful geometric designs into which bushels of noodles could disappear.

Brigitte Webb of Dingwall, Scotland, is among the most creative (and funny) of noodle-user-uppers I have ever met. We only wish we could show you all of the rugs in which Brigette has used her noodles in creative ways. Lori Stopak, a quilter-turned-hooker, is attracted to the patchwork designs in antique rugs. As she considered reupholstering a family heirloom, her mind turned to her tub of noodles. She ended up hooking the covering for the bench and reducing her noodle inventory by about three-quarters. It's difficult to imagine a more suitable design for this simple bench.

Have a look at these creative examples. Then grab the sketchbook and doodle away on your own noodle designs.

Hair to Dye For, *18" x 18", #3-, 4-, 5-, and 6-cut wool and bits of yarn on monks cloth. Designed and hooked by Brigitte Webb, Dingwall, Scotland, 2010.*

"Never having had any formal drawing lessons," Brigitte said, "and reading that if one tried and kept practicing, improvements could be achieved, I thought I would give it a try. Nothing ventured, nothing gained. This was my first attempt at drawing and hooking a face.

"Having an enormous stash of multicolored strips of wool (worms), I had the idea of using some of these to create the hair. The title pun came into my mind, and the design evolved from that thought. I love movement in designs. After I drew the head shape and the features, I added a few squiggly lines and curls for the hair. The eyes, nose, and mouth were hooked first, proving to me I had much to learn still. Then I started hooking the shapes in the hair using my worms.

"Before starting, I thought this would be the easy part of the rug. But as with all hooked rugs, it required a balance of color and texture. As one may notice in much of my work, I do love bright happy colors."

OPPOSITE PAGE: Scrappy Pew, *62" x 31", #8-cut wool on linen. Designed and hooked by Lori Stopak, Council Bluffs, Iowa, 2016.*

This old bench had been in Lori's in-laws' basement for as long as she could remember. "They got some water in the basement," she said, "and had to move it to the wall with things around it, so it sat there for another decade. It's not long enough to be a regular church pew, but it may have been up near the lectern for the priest to sit on. My father-in-law passed away, and eventually the kids got around to disposing of things. This bench was about to be pitched if no one wanted it. I pounced!

"It sat in my sewing room with a throw over it, since there were big holes ripped in the seat. I asked for upholstery suggestions, but wasn't thrilled with the ideas of animal fur or teal leather. Finally I decided to use up the two large tubs of noodles in my sewing room closet. I did have to cut a few orange and purple strips to include in each square, but my stash of noodles has diminished to about half of one small tote. Charles Tornblom did the upholstery work for me and he was very excited to have an unusual project to work on. He said it took him about 20 hours to build up the seat and stabilize the frame of the piece. He was as happy as I with the final product."

Scraps, *18" x 14", #3-, 4-, 5-, 6-, and 7-cut wool on monk's cloth. Designed and hooked by Brigitte Webb, Dingwall, Scotland, 2008.*

"In hooking this small rug," Brigitte said, "I wanted to use my ever-growing supply of bits and strips of wool. I made it as a gift for my eldest son's fiancée, who adores cats. I drew directly onto the monk's cloth with my black Sharpie. Alterations and mistakes are always covered up with hooking—in my case a good thing.

"I hooked it almost like a child would draw and colour, so there was no colour-planning involved. I started by hooking the eyes, nose, and mouth, then the rest of the head. The body was great fun to do, as was the tail. For the background, I used several small pieces of black wools of varying values, perhaps reminiscent of folks in days gone by who hooked with whatever they could find."

Start with Materials 107

Design Idea #6: Mix of Textile Arts

She seeketh wool and flax and worketh willingly with her hands.
—Proverbs 31:13

Fallen Leaves, *11" x 11", #4-cut wool on linen. Designed and hooked by Val Flannigan, Kelowna, British Columbia, 2013.*

"This design was based on a piece of spot-dyed wool," said Val. "In order to make the most out of the wool, I hooked it sequentially. This was not the effect I wanted, as I thought it looked like a very mushy background. Then I had the idea of adding some felt leaves, in similar colors, which I then felted on. For an additional layer, I used various colors of embroidery floss to add random seed stitches on the leaves. Then looking at the piece, I saw that some of the sequential hooking was reversed. I decided that I could reduce this by adding beads, in the same color family, in cascading lines. I found this incredible yarn in the same colors, so I had to try the crocheted edge. This piece totally evolved on its own."

Some of us have all we can handle with one fiber art. Our spaces are full of the relevant tools and materials needed for hooking.

But we all know someone, don't we, who is an omnivorous fiber artist? Sure, she hooks. But she also felts and does wool appliqué and embroiders and attends the monthly gatherings of her quilting group. I have such friends. My Danish friend, Karen Marie Greenfield, is one of these miraculous ambi-fibrous artists. At a very young age, her parents taught her to knit, crochet, and make dolls. She does needle felting, and she appliqués with extraordinary skill and precision. Of course she dyes wool, silk, yarns, and other fibers. This design idea is for people like Karen, but we hope it will entice others to expand their textile expertise.

Consider mixing textile arts with hooking in order to add a whole new dimension of creativity. Val Flannigan was inspired by a piece of wool, but ended up using several textiles and methods along with hooking to create *Fallen Leaves*. Kay LeFevre created the perfect design for hooking tulle tutus into her mat. Diane Cox has been collecting fabrics for years: old tablecloths, cushion covers, and antique quilts. In her hooking projects, Diane has used appliqué and embroidery to incorporate lovely vintage textiles into her work, with wonderful results.

For those who are inspired by what you see here, I must recommend an old book that is out of print: *Quilting, Patchwork, Appliqué, and Trapunto: Traditional Methods and Original Designs*, by Thelma R. Newman. Published in 1974, this volume is filled with diagrams and photographs, detailed descriptions, and how-to assistance. Look for it with used booksellers online. You may find it instructive, but at the very least, you will take inspiration from the fiber artists on its pages.

As an antique textile collector, I own some falling-apart quilts which I have hoped to preserve somehow. After seeing the work of Diane Cox, it occurs to me that the best parts of these old quilts could live on for decades if I followed Diane's example, incorporating pieces into a rug design.

Granny Angel, 30" x 56", *recycled fabrics, chenille yarn, and sheep's fleece on hessian backing, with embroidery on vintage fabrics. Designed and hooked by Diane Cox, Penzance, Cornwall, 2015.*

"Many years ago," Diane said, "I painted a small picture of an old lady with long skirts hiding pockets full of interesting things. I had this in mind when our group decided to hook our own angel rugs. I had recently acquired three new grandsons in one year, so my mind was full of being a granny. This rug emerged.

"From my sketches, I drew a simple figure and decided to use fabric for the skirt. The detail I wanted to put into the skirt was easier for me to do this way, and also the vintage fabrics I used reminded me of my own childhood and grandmothers. The backing behind the pink skirt fabric is a lovely old soft wool blanket. It was really pleasant to sew through. The stitching took me quite a long time to finish, and I worked on this first before starting the hooking.

"My own grandmothers were creative, hardworking, loving, and patient, and I was thinking of them all the time I made this piece, hoping that my own grandchildren will have good memories of me."

Keeping an Eye Out, 18" x 23", *recycled fabrics and wool yarn on hessian backing, with embroidery on vintage textiles. Designed and hooked by Diane Cox, Penzance, Cornwall, 2014.*

"I made this rug in response to my husband losing the sight in one eye," Diane said. "He lost it overnight, and not only did it allow me to express my feelings, but the process of hooking kept me calm during months of operations and hospital visits. I knew I wanted to hook half a face, to represent the one good eye, but I also wanted to put words into the piece. Appliqué and embroidery were easier than hooking for this, as the rug is fairly small.

"'Do what you can with what you have, where you are' is a favorite saying of mine and always helps me through difficult times. I like the odd shapes of vintage fabrics and stitching in this because life just isn't neat and tidy."

Start with Materials **109**

7
Start with a Story

Setting Out, *10½" x 13", #4-cut wool on linen. Designed and hooked by Ann Willey, Comstock Park, Michigan, 2004.*

"The image sprung from my fascination with the Persephone/Demeter story of Greek mythology," Ann said. "Demeter's daughter Persephone is taken to the Underworld by Hades. Persephone leaves her mother's home, taking the promise of warmth and flowers with her and moves alone into a shadowy world. Demeter grieves her loss and allows the world to become barren while she is gone.

"Setting Out *is about that pivotal moment in so many stories, when the heroine takes up her destiny and ventures into the unknown. This resonated in my life at the time. My youngest child was leaving the nest and taking off into the big, bad world on her own. She struggled, but like Persephone, emerged intact and whole.*"

As a long-ago student of storytelling, I learned about the elements of a narrative. Every story has a setting—its place and time—along with its characters and events. Our story rugs may focus on one or more of these elements, depending on what is most important to us.

Home and Other Places

Places can garner our affections almost as much as people can. Often a story rug will simply show the beauty of a place we love, whether it be a familiar room, house, or landscape, an ancestral homeland, or a vacation destination we wish to capture. Don't be surprised if, like John Flournoy, you start seeing rugs everyplace you look: intricate Victorian houses require a different kind of attention than humble old barns and fields, but both evoke a longing for the past.

Nostalgia for Another Time

Many of us carry memories of a time when life seemed simpler, happier, and better. There are many ways to convey our fondness for these memories in our rugs. Some rug hooking teachers are experts at ways of hooking nostalgia into every loop, giving them a vintage feeling through our colors and values, or through the retro components in the patterns we draw.

*I believe in stories, in their incredible power
to keep people alive, to keep the living alive, and the dead.*

—Tim O'Brien

The Big Catch, *18" x 22", #3-cut wool on linen. Designed and hooked by John Flournoy, Lewes, Delaware, 2005.*

This rug features John's father on a fishing trip. "I found the photo in the family album long after he had passed away," John said. "I never knew my father as a fisherman. During my childhood, he was always a hunter."

The Characters of Our Lives

We could hook all our days and not capture all of our dear ones. Nuclear family members, grandchildren, fast friends, and even ancestors whom we've never met may become the subjects of our rug designs, to say nothing of the furry and feathered creatures who also keep us company. Portrait rugs are lovely, but remember also the value of capturing someone's familiar posture, her gestures, her wide-brimmed hat and gardening shoes. Some of the most interesting story rugs show their subjects in profile, from behind, at work or at rest in his or her favorite setting.

Events to Remember

We naturally want to commemorate formal occasions, the milestones of our lives, like marriages, births, graduations and other accomplishments, and retirements. But sometimes the occasion you want to remember is an ordinary moment. My parents, whose house was sheltered by old oak trees, used to spend their autumn Sundays raking, and this humble activity was an annual event that I once captured in a rug.

This chapter suggests six design ideas for telling your own stories in a rug.

Design Idea #1: Where We Come From

*Home is a place you grow up wanting to leave
and grow old wanting to get back to.*

—John Ed Pearce

For many years, our parents have owned a cabin on a quiet Minnesota lake, and my siblings and I share those memories—boating and fishing memories, painting and fix-up memories, and rainy-day memories of looking out at the gray lake and curling up with a good book. I have hooked it twice—once drawing a simple postcard picture of the cabin at sunset as the surface of the lake turned pink and lavender. I also hooked a great blue heron standing among the cattails, a familiar sight at our family cabin. I have more cabin rugs to hook—a green kayak creating ripples on still water, the weathered planks of an old dock, and turtles sunning themselves on the rocks along the shore. As my friend Roslyn Logsdon has said, "There are so many angles to view the world."

This design challenge is an invitation to hook your own familiar place: a landscape, a front door, a garden, a street scene, a family business, or even an ancestral homeland.

Some of us lived in a single home-place for our entire childhoods, while others may have moved during childhood from place to place. In any case, there were certain possessions, gathering places, recurring moments that meant "home" to us. My mother's large family was dirt poor and moved often when she was a child, but home was always a pump spewing cold well water and some chickens in the yard. Three times a day, Grandma made biscuits, scooping flour from her barrel and sifting it before kneading her dough. The flour barrel and the sifter meant home to my mother.

Denise Hoffman has hooked many rugs to depict the Nebraska ranch where she grew up. She has hooked cows, horses, chickens, and cowboy boots. Recently she hooked her parents in their younger days, at the screen door of the family home. But to add to her gallery of home-place rugs, she wrote to artist P. Buckley Moss for permission to adapt a painting of the prairie in winter, entitled *Blessed Peace*. "When I look at P. Buckley Moss's art," Denise said, "she always draws me back to the peace and serenity of my rural heritage. I can almost smell the crisp wintery air."

We can draw our images from a single address, from familiar possessions, from family photos, or even from the work of another artist. Consider the places of importance in your life, and create your own memory rug.

St. Agnes by the Sea, *39" x 22", #3-cut wool on linen. Adapted from an old sepia postcard. Designed and hooked by John Flournoy, Lewes, Delaware 2008.*

John has hooked many rugs that preserve images of elegant old homes, architecturally special places, and landmarks of Rehoboth Beach, Delaware. The town is very special to John, and he is particularly fond of older structures, finding them "more appealing to hook. I like the many details, the gingerbread, clapboard siding, and screen porches," he said.

Perhaps the best-known rug of the Rehoboth Beach series is John's Celebration winner, Saint Agnes by the Sea, a serenely intricate adaptation of an old sepia postcard, complete with the 1911 postmark and the sender's casual handwritten message. This church, St. Agnes, used to sit just above the ocean on the dunes at the center of the village. Rehoboth Beach is still a very popular resort community, but with so much development, John continues to hook the older buildings before they are lost to "progress."

Grandmother's House, *37" x 40", #8-cut wool on linen. Designed and hooked by Holly McMillan, Roca, Nebraska, 2015.*

"My teacher was known for house rugs," Holly said, "and my favorite house in memory was Grandma Glidden's. It was a Victorian style with several small porches and lots of pretty trim.

"I made the house a quiet, soft spot for the eye to settle on. We spent many summers out in that yard. Grandma was so proud of her flowers. She liked a lot of traditional old-fashioned flowers, as we call them now. Even the alley was planted with flowers, and if you grew up in a small midwestern town, you know hollyhocks often lined the alleys. The picture I used for the hollyhocks was taken in an alley here in Lincoln, so some things never change. She even adorned her clothesline with morning glory, and I did dye the colors for these myself. I hope I did her proud. My favorite nemesis was the mulberry tree on the corner. It was always staining my feet purple, because I was barefoot a lot, even with the sandburs. I initially wanted just a purple shadow to signify the staining, but opted for a much more whimsical way to do that, hooking the trunk purple, blue, and even pink.

"For me, it was important that the house be encompassed by the flowers and the tree, as if to protect it from time. I went back to take pictures of it and was devastated by how it looks now. I prefer my memory of it. I sent the rug to the Nebraska State Fair. Some relatives were looking for my rugs, but they said the labels were hard to read. They found mine, as they recognized Grandma's house."

Design Idea #2: Milestones

Cherish all your happy moments.
They make a fine cushion for old age.

—Booth Tarkington

Adaptation of Christian, 30" x 23", #3- and 4-cut wool on linen. Adapted with permission from a photo by James Cattlett. Designed and hooked by Jodi Isom, Lincoln, Nebraska, 2014. JAMES CATTLETT

Sometimes we celebrate our own milestones by hooking a rug, but in Jodi's case, she celebrated her nephew's college graduation. Jodi saw a photo of Christian, featuring his outstanding Mohawk, and decided to adapt and hook it in a workshop with Donna Hrkman. Although she had always worked in wider cuts of wool, she accepted the challenge of using #3- and 4-cut wool for this rug. Her favorite part is the "flaming" Mohawk, which Christian had to cut upon his college graduation. The rug is his now, a reminder of his college days and the generosity of his aunt.

When Jodi's rug won inclusion in Celebration 2015, the judges called it "a unique monochromatic rug with a surprising bright touch, interesting contrasts, and a dramatic mixing of neutrals and bold colors."

I once commemorated an accomplishment of a family member who after many years of struggle achieved a first year of sobriety. The rug's design was the image of a raven on a branch, with leaves swirling all around, which for us symbolized staying grounded when the world feels chaotic. In the border, in a subtle, low-contrast way, I hooked three key words from The Prayer of St. Francis: serenity, courage, and wisdom.

The important occasions of our lives and the lives of those close to us can become our reasons for designing and hooking a special rug. Anniversaries, retirements, birthdays, and holidays are by definition formal milestones in our lives. But I encourage you to think about other events that feel like a beginning of something promising or a conclusion of something important. At times when a simple goal is accomplished, when a challenge is overcome, when we move house or change jobs, or when beloved people join us or leave us, we can be inspired to commemorate the occasion through creative expression.

Our sketchbooks will serve us well at such times, when our creative expression might take many different forms. First, settle on one occasion that is a milestone for you or for someone important to you. Don't stop at one sketch. Keep going until your imagination is exhausted, and then look back at your sketches and mull over your options.

Long before I started rug hooking, my brother earned a

Two Crows, Joy, *28" x 36", #7- through 8.5-cut wool on linen. Designed and hooked by Tamara Pavich, Council Bluffs, Iowa, 2011.* PETER C. PHILLIPS

I made this rug for someone very dear to me. I'm happy to say that he has stayed true to himself, has built a supportive community, and has redeemed his life and talents from the grip of addiction. He is living the good life he deserves.

Newborn Twins, *30" x 18", yarn on rug warp. Designed and hooked by Kay LeFevre, Windsor, Ontario, Canada, 2012.*

"I made this for a co-worker who had twins," Kay said, "using colors from her nursery. I used a photo she sent me, and the hardest part was finding the right color for the babies' flesh. I think I bought five wrong colors before I settled on this one. I still search for the perfect skin tones. This was not a detailed portrait, just a simple outline sketch of each of the babies. She was thrilled with it and still talks about it to this day. Giving rugs is such a wonderful thing to do for people who appreciate it.

master's degree in tree-ring studies, and his research required him to core over 200 trees. I could have commemorated this milestone in his life with a landscape of the woodland he studied, with a closeup of the tree-rings themselves, or a botanical design, showing the leaves and acorns of an indigenous oak species. Just thinking through these potential designs makes me want to hook a belated "congratulations rug," just 15 years after he completed his master's project.

Has someone in your circle of friends completed a marathon, finished a community service project, or checked something off the bucket list? Has a friend come through a difficult medical challenge? In addition to taking inspiration from the accomplishments of your friends and family, consider hooking your own milestone rug. If you begin practicing yoga, hook your favorite posture. If your retirement is approaching, hook your desires for your new life chapter into a rug. Before long, you will begin to see every significant event as a story rug that preserves and celebrates the experience. It takes many rugs to chronicle our lives. Better start designing.

Start with a Story

Design Idea #3: Family Lore

Even with different sides of the same story, there is still agreement that this is the family story.

—Amy M. Homes

I am blessed with a colorful family history. Another way to say that is that some members of our family did some pretty crazy stuff. When he was just a teenager, my grandfather decided to make some extra money. Times were tough, and one dark night, he and his brothers tossed bags of cash off a moving train and later ran back to retrieve them. He spent five years in prison for the crime.

It seems like it would take Steven Spielberg and all of his major-motion-picture resources to tell that story. But in our story rugs, we aim to simplify these tales, reduce them to a single frame that captures a moment in our family's history.

Telling stories can be a way to savor good memories or maybe to make peace with not-so-good memories. My mother had a difficult childhood, picking cotton in the sweltering fields of Arkansas when she was very young. When I hooked that scene of my mom as a child in the field, it turned painful memories into better ones by honoring her difficult early life. While I hooked the rug, my mother and my aunt began to talk about what it was like, coming home from the hot field to a house without air conditioning. "We didn't even have a fan!" my aunt said, laughing. "Not even screens to keep the mosquitoes out," my mother said. For Mom, I think the rug is a celebration of her survival of those years. (See *Lilly in the Field* on page 124.)

Your challenge will be to hone in on one scene or element in the story and draw that. Photographs may or may not exist, and you may need to employ a great deal of imagination to put your story into a picture. Talk to the members of your family about the details they remember. Condense, condense, condense. Use symbols to help convey meaning. Construct a scene, simple or complex, that tells your family's story. It may be as simple as the moon shining down on an open satchel of cash beside railroad tracks.

Tree House, *32" x 39", #8-cut on linen. Adapted from a family photo. Designed and hooked by Lilly Phillips, Council Bluffs, Iowa, 2015.* PETER C. PHILLIPS

The old photo that inspired this rug was filled with yellow sunlight. Lilly's four children lined up in their tree house, Lori, Dave, Pete, and the oldest, Tammy (Tamara Phillips Pavich) on the left, holding the family dog, Princess. "We moved here when our four children were small," Lilly said, "with acres of woods behind the house. Jim built the tree house in 1970. We took pictures, and they have been in our photo box for 45 years. It was a wonderful fun time. The kids slept out there, ate lunch there. Even our neighbor boy, Chris, now a 52-year-old man, still tells stories about the tree house."

OPPOSITE PAGE: Eden's Garden, *35" x 27", #7-, 8-, and 8.5-cut wool on linen. Designed and hooked by Terri Bangert, Lincoln, Nebraska, 2015.*

"I was registered for a workshop with Pris Buttler at Star of Texas. I wanted to challenge myself to design, but as the day approached, I began to feel more and more intimidated, my thoughts swirling with 'I can't draw,' 'I have no idea about design,' and 'what was I thinking?' Then it came to me--my father's garden. Very quickly, Pris got me to tell my story, coached me to just let my hand be free to draw. Her artistic skills were needed, though, specifically on the squirrel!

"*Eden's Garden* depicts our backyard growing up. In the winter months, my dad would receive seed catalogs in the mail. He and Mom would select what they would plant each year, which vegetables for the garden, which flowers for the borders and pots. Each little seed pampered under his system of grow-lights, watering, and nurturing.

"The red bud tree welcomed the birds, and the antique bird bath would bring splashing joy all year round, because of the heating element placed by Dad. The flowers were all brought to glorious vibrancy under his green thumb. A separate corner of the backyard held the rose garden. I remember the gentle fragrance in our home, roses floating in water. The comical squirrels taunted Dad, stealing seed from his bird feeders. We were blessed to actually have the white picket fence, though I didn't think so when it came time to repaint it."

Design Idea #4: Remembering You

In this life, I was loved by you.

—Israel Kamakawiwo'ole

Remembering Ann, *32" x 27", #5- through 8-cut wool on linen. Designed and hooked by Tamara Pavich, Council Bluffs, Iowa, 2014.* PETER C. PHILLIPS

Donna Hrkman was my teacher on this rug, my first-ever realistic portrait, hooked for my mother after the death of Aunt Ann. I placed many symbols of their lifelong friendship in the rug. I believe Donna could help anyone hook a realistic portrait. She explains things in ways that are easy to understand and do, and she offers continual encouragement.

I once visited the studio of Rhonda Manley, protégé of the late Emma Lou Lais. There were so many rugs to see, but I was struck by the simplest design in the middle of the floor. A large circular rug was filled with the motif of a primitive weeping willow tree, its branches bending low with leaves of various greens and browns. The wording said simply, "Dad, Remembered."

Use this design idea in whatever way feels right for you. Hooking a symbol of sadness (the weeping willow) may be the best way to soothe a loss. And there are other beautiful memory rugs that conjure the essence of a loved one in associated scenes or motifs. Pat Shafer's award-winning rug celebrated her late son's love of music in a riot of multicolored piano keys. Terri Bangert's *Eden's Garden*, featured in these pages, depicts her father's garden.

Though we often imagine remembering someone with a portrait, there are other approaches for designing a remembrance rug. Perhaps envision your dear one at a distance, his distinctive posture, her clothing, the tilt of the head or folded hands. Place your neighbor or grandparent in his or her favorite setting. She may be facing a window watching snowfall, or he could be at a distance, driving a favorite old car.

Hi Daddy, I'm Sophie, *36" x 26", #3- and 4-cut wool and miscellaneous fibers on cotton rug warp. Designed and hooked by Marilyn Becker, Wausau, Wisconsin, 2015.*

"About two years ago," Marilyn said, "my husband was diagnosed with Lewy Body Dementia disease, very similar to Alzheimer's disease. Soon after, our little Schnauzer, Sophie, crawled up on his chest and looked at him as she has done many times before. I had to capture this moment in a photo. A year later, I decided to hook this experience in a rug for remembrance.

"It's not easy to make faces look like the person you are portraying. We have been married 56 years, and I didn't want to see someone else's face on my rug. So I started by hooking the dark parts of his face, then the lighter, then filled in with medium-value colors, always using the photo as a guide. Sophie was easy—all hair.

"A quilt I made with prominent hexagons hangs behind my husband's chair. My friend Cathy Stephan asked, "Are you going to hook the hexagons?" It was a good idea, and I cut patterns of hexagons out of plastic and traced them onto the background. From my worm basket, I pulled all the various colors. That was fun."

We needn't be afraid of portraits, though. Faces certainly can be a challenge at first, but everything improves with practice. Be sure to consult Anne Marie Littenberg's excellent book on hooking portraits. After practicing on my own, a class with Donna Hrkman helped me greatly, and I continue to study and practice portraits with her and other teachers.

In my rug *Remembering Ann* I wanted to help my mom with the loss of Aunt Ann. Mom and Ann were kids together, and though the miles separated them, they spent hours on the telephone, sent care packages wrapped in brown paper, and shared hundreds of cups of strong coffee during their visits, which became more frequent during Ann's illness. With her portrait at the center, I added the two telephones to the design, along with a pair of coffee mugs and a care package. In the background, I drew figure eights and distorted hearts on the linen and hooked them into the design. I wanted those symbols of love and infinity in the rug, because their friendship stays alive with my mother, even after Ann's death. In the border, I placed Ann's name and the dates of her life, as well as the words to a favorite song: "In this life, I was loved by you." The rug hangs at Mom's bedside.

Design Idea #5: Featured Creature

I have been studying the traits and dispositions of the "lower animals" and contrasting them with the traits and dispositions of man. I find the result humiliating to me.

—Mark Twain

Olifant, 18" x 20", #4-cut on linen. Designed and hooked by Val Flannigan, Kelowna, British Columbia, 2012.
"This piece was designed from a photo that my son had taken on a family holiday in a game park in South Africa," Val said. "I had his permission to adapt it to a rug. As in starting a portrait, I began with the eye, which I later took out and decided to sculpt it for a better effect. I did my own dyeing but used this wonderful wool that had different textures on either side. The background color was chosen to compliment the dusty and hot environment."

During the winter months, four deer come out of the woods and into the Phillips's yard every night. They stand near the tall kitchen windows until Lilly scoops corn from a bucket and carries it out to the feeder. The deer don't run from her anymore; they wait patiently for her to step back so they can eat. Sometimes, after supper, they lie down near the woodpile at the edge of the woods.

Lilly has never taken a rug-hooking class, but has forged ahead into designing her own rugs since the day she picked up a hook. She breaks rules, lets the design drip over onto the border of the rug, and trusts that wool will transform a simple design into a memory from her life. Her depiction of the deer in the woods was perhaps the fourth rug she designed and hooked. (See her rug, *Deer*, on pages 34-35.)

As you pause in our chapter on story, please consider the animals, wild or domesticated, that have somehow touched your life. Images of cattle and horses resonate for my friend Denise because she grew up on a Nebraska ranch. Gail Dufresne has become famous in the rug-hooking world for her delightful and colorful hooked goats and reptiles. My friend Jane Scott is as fond of birds as I am and has hooked her share of glorious bird species. Many rug hookers who

Tedy, *12 ½" x 16", #4-cut on linen. Designed and hooked by Val Flannigan, Kelowna, British Columbia, 2015.*

"For an upcoming class with Diane Phillips called Dog Portrait in a Day," Val said, "I went to some photos that I had taken of my youngest Airedale. She has such a personality and an attitude that I wanted to convey. I had several great photos of her and chose this one to base my pattern on. One ear always manages to flip up and she gets this wild look in her eyes and often gets referred to as my wild child. Cropping the pattern adds to the overall effectiveness of catching the essence of this beloved pet."

have never left the United States enjoy hooking images of exotic animals like big cats, pachyderms, or giraffes.

We infer meaning for some animals; they are symbols for us. We automatically think about persistence when we see the plodding turtle. The owl seems to peer at us in silent wisdom. A fluffy lamb epitomizes innocence and vulnerability. I happen to love pigs, probably because they are associated with my home state, Iowa. But after hooking many plump pink pigs, it's interesting to learn that they are symbols of prosperity and abundance.

The nearest and dearest animals in our lives, of course, are our pets. They enrich our days, make us laugh, and bring companionship into our homes. When we lose them, we want to find a way to keep their essence with us. Who among us has not hooked her beloved pet into a rug?

Certain teachers/authors in the rug hooking community have distinguished themselves in the area of hooking animal images: Judy Carter and Jon Ciemiewicz, for instance. Judy's book is an animal encyclopedia: lions, tigers, bears, oh my! As you think about furry friends and acquaintances, remember that many teachers can help you with your first animal rug design.

Design Idea #6: Sepia Memento

se·pi·a *(sē'pē-ə) n. a) A dark brown ink or pigment originally prepared from the secretion of the cuttlefish. b) A drawing or picture done in this pigment. c) A photograph in a brown tint.*

—*Webster's Dictionary*

Rendering an old photo in sepia wool can be challenging, but it may be one of the most rewarding rugs you ever hook. Surely you've seen some of the best examples of this genre in *Rug Hooking* magazine and in the pages of *Celebration*. Here are some suggestions on designing and hooking a sepia memento of your own.

Sepia Photo Technology

Software for digital cameras or for printers, or even your photocopy store, can help you turn any photo into a sepia-toned "antique."

Composite Images

Even if you don't possess the exact photo you wish to hook, be resourceful and combine images that reflect your memory or story. From the Internet, I collected photos of cotton fields like the ones in which my mother worked as a child. Cathy Stephan drew the pattern, placing my mother's youthful figure in such a field. While hooking, I continually referred to these photos to shade the face, dress, cotton sack, and landscape.

Your Sepia Palette

Among the examples included here, you will notice slight variations in color palettes. Marilyn Becker's sepia palette leans to pink. The palette of *Lilly in the Field* includes grayish tones along with the browns. Whatever sepia palette you choose—goldish brown, reddish brown, gray and brown--remain faithful to it throughout the project.

Light Source and Shadow

In almost any photo, you will notice the way shadows fall. If the face is lighter on the left than on the right, your light source is shining from the left, leaving the right in shadow. The foreground is usually lighter, with higher contrast, and the background is darker, with lower contrast.

Smaller Cuts

The rugs featured here range from #3-cut to #8.5-cut, and certainly the wider cuts, hooked with patience and skill, can result in a realistic image. Depending on the size of your rug and the detail in your photograph, though, you may have to adjust your normal cut to something smaller. Especially for facial detail, use the appropriate cut. Your rug will be better for it.

Organizing Your Shades of Brown

Cathy Stephan points out that when you're hooking a winter sky, a white house, two faces, and a lot of snow, as in Cathy's student, Marilyn Becker's beautiful rug, you will need to create and follow a scheme, using many light values. For flesh tones especially, you'll be cutting strips of wool that are almost indistinguishable from each other. Don't mix them all together; rather, find a way to keep your strips in order, from light to dark. You may use a noodle organizer or a strip of masking tape that holds everything to its position on the spectrum. You may even find it useful to assign numbers to your shades of brown, from the lightest shade up through the darker ones. Strictly sorting and labeling your strips will help you incorporate many different wools of similar value into a comprehensible picture.

Likeness, Rather than Perfection

You can do this. Gather your sepia wools, and use the suggestions in Chapter 2 to draw your image on the linen. You may not end up with an exact replica of your photo, but you will have a likeness. Do your best work, and decide when to be satisfied with this sepia effort. Then move on to the next.

Cathy Stephan's Sepia Dye Recipe

Sepia Dye
½ tsp. Canary
5/64 + 1/128 tsp. Cherry
1/16 + 1/128 tsp. Peacock
3/64 tsp. Black

Cathy used Cushing dyes. She tore the fat quarters of Dorr Natural wool into three long pieces for 1/12-yard pieces. Use the dye in these amounts for her gradations of color:

- 1 tsp. dye over 1/12 yard
- 2 tsp. dye over 1/12 yard
- 4 tsp. dye over 1/12 yard
- 6 tsp. dye over 1/12 yard
- 8 tsp. dye over 1/12 yard
- 10 tsp. dye over 1/12 yard
- 12 tsp. dye over 1/12 yard

"When I was dyeing for snow background, I used half-yard pieces and used six times the lighter value amounts. To add variation, I used a light camel herringbone and a tiny, light taupe texture for the shadows in Marilyn's snow." (*Marry Me, Mary*).

O Captain! My Captain!, *19" x 22", #3- through 8.5-cuts wool on rug warp. Designed and hooked by Cathy Stephan, Athens, Wisconsin, 2013.*

This rug shares its title with the Walt Whitman poem about President Abraham Lincoln. "This was the last known picture of him," Cathy said, "taken late in his life, and it is plain to see the weariness and sorrow etched into his features. My husband and I have a charcoal sketch of him on our parlor wall. President Lincoln always carried himself nobly, and his great sorrow was for the young men who died in battle. He tried to offer comfort to countless mothers of fallen soldiers who came to the White House to see him."

Start with a Story

(Sepia Memento continued)

One Crow, Sorrow, *19" x 22 ½", #7-, 8-, and 8.5-cut wool on linen. Adapted with permission from the sepia photograph, "Her Graveyard," by Donna Snyder. Designed and hooked by Tamara Pavich, Council Bluffs, Iowa, 2013.*

"I hooked the figure of the crow first, but felt disappointed that the subtle contrasts in my browns didn't show up well at all. But as I completed the headstones, branches, background, and border, the appearance of the crow changed, gaining dimension and detail. It's important to remember that with every additional element, the rug keeps changing in significant ways."

Lilly in the Field, *37" x 39", #5-, 6-, 8-, and 8.5-cuts, wool on linen. Designed by Cathy Stephan and Tamara Pavich. Hooked by Tamara Pavich, Council Bluffs, Iowa, 2013.*

"My mother, Lilly Yarbrough, grew up in Arkansas, and as a child she worked in the cotton fields. She would have been 11 in 1949; hence, the date on her cotton sack. The minute I spoke to Cathy Stephan about this project, she became as enthusiastic as I was about it. On day two of the workshop, I had to let go a little and accept that I was capturing the spirit of my mom's childhood, if not every detail of her young face. I once read a poem about the daytime moon, waiting off stage for her moment to shine. I hooked a sliver of a daytime moon in the sky of this picture as a symbol of my mom during her difficult early life."

Marry Me, Mary, *36" x 48", #3- to 6-cut repurposed wool and yarn on rug warp. Adapted from a family photograph. Designed and hooked by Marilyn Becker, Wausau, Wisconsin, 2013.*

"My sister found a box of old photos that my mom had stored away," Marilyn said. "In 1928, Mom was only 15 years old, and Dad had just inherited the farm on which they had built their beautiful new house. I bottle fed many spring lambs on this farm, and my brothers and sisters and I grew up under wool blankets and comforters made from the virgin wool of our sheep. We learned to appreciate wool during our cold Wisconsin winters."

Marilyn's father's shirt is hooked in wool from his own shirt, which she kept after he passed away. "I hooked Mom's fur collar and cuffs in eyelash yarn. Note the hole in Mom's stocking knee. The everyday stockings were made of soft, heavy cotton. That's the reason the hole shows up so well."

Mary Rose, *32" x 58", #3- and 4-cut wool on cotton rug warp. Adapted from a family photograph. Designed and hooked by Marilyn Becker, Wausau, Wisconsin, 2014. This rug is a* Celebration *winner of 2015.*

"This rug is adapted from a photo taken in 1918 of my mother, Mary Rose, at age five," Marilyn said. "I love the sepia color of old photos and wanted to try to replicate it in my rug, except for the ribbon on her dress, which I wanted to be rose colored to honor her name."

Marilyn's process began with the natural dyeing of various wools with black walnuts. The degree of her faithfulness to every detail in this rug is astonishing, and at Sauder Village, where her award-winning rug was displayed, Marilyn was surrounded by admirers.

She describes the techniques she used to mimic the dress fabric alone: "Eyelet is characterized by holes in the fabric, so you can see the background through it. I used white and dark brown wool, hooking one stitch white, one stitch brown. When I came to the daisies, I drew circles in their place and finished the rest of the rug. I tried many ways of hooking the daisies with several different cuts of wool. I wasn't satisfied. Then my daughter suggested making cocoons of wool and sewing them to the backing. I used to do embroidery and remembered the bullion stitch. After many attempts, it began to satisfy me. I made pompoms for the center of the daisy and sewed on the woolen bullion cocoons (10 cocoon petals to each daisy) with thread and needle. I also hooked the background and in between the daisies in light, shadowy pink."

Start with a Story

8

Start with You

Be yourself. Everyone else is already taken.

—Oscar Wilde

Snowy Sisters, 8¾" x 8¾", #4-cut wool on linen. Designed and hooked by Trish Johnson, Toronto, Ontario, 2008.

"This is my home," Trish said, "my roots: small town, Northern Ontario. The air is crisp and dry. The sky is cloudless and blue. The snow sparkles. The temperature is minus 40 degrees Fahrenheit. This is my sister and me. For five years I was an only child, and I really wanted a sister or maybe twin brothers. I am glad to have a sister now. She is my friend. I made this little rug to commemorate a time when we were cute and little."

Way back in Chapter 1, we said, "If you're reading this book, then you probably wish to find and express meaning in your life." Of course, in some way or other, everything we hook is a meaningful reflection of ourselves. Even when we hook something that we didn't design, our own tastes and delights come through in our color choices and our manner of hooking.

But the potential for self-expression grows immensely as we begin to design. This book has offered ways of designing around a new style, a color palette, works of art, the materials we use, and stories--our own or the stories of others. Of course, all of these design ideas stimulate questions: *What attracts me? What do I find exciting or interesting? What do I value? What do I have to give or express? What do I desire to record and preserve? What is here inside me, wanting to come out?*

In this, our final chapter, we invite our readers to design rugs around themselves—their own beliefs and ideas, their

Contentment, 44" x 45", *recycled fabrics and sheep's fleece on hessian backing. Designed and hooked by Diane Cox, Penzance, Cornwall, 2011.*

For Diane, this was a purely personal piece. "It's very large," she said, "containing the things that make me feel contented. The things shown are all simple, domestic, and cozy. It rains a lot in Cornwall, and I wanted to show a grey, drizzly day outside, because I love those days too.

"From time to time, I put this rug aside, and it took three years to complete. When I started, I only had one dog, so midway through I had to add our little white terrier. Luckily there was space in the picture . . . on my lap! During the hooking, my black cat with one white whisker died, but a few years later, we gave a home to another black cat. I have Contentment *hanging in my sitting room.*"

everyday lives, the causes that matter to them, their histories, and their very identities. When we find a subject that matters deeply to us, we sometimes wish to make more than one attempt at expressing or depicting it; therefore, series of rugs can be born, in which we pursue the same subject from various angles or perspectives until the lesson is complete—or at least until we're ready to move on. And finally, if we seek the most literal meaning of self-expression, a self-portrait can result. In my research for this book, I continually broadened my idea of what a self-portrait can be, and the final design idea in this chapter will suggest at least a few ways of approaching such a project, from realism to caricature and more.

In a recent letter from Diane Cox, she wrote, "I can't do a rug these days without it being very personal or a form of self-exploration." We wish you the curiosity and the freedom to embark on your own journey. May we all take our favorite fiber art to new levels of self-expression in our own unique ways.

Design Idea #1: I Believe

Create beauty every day.
—Deanne Fitzpatrick

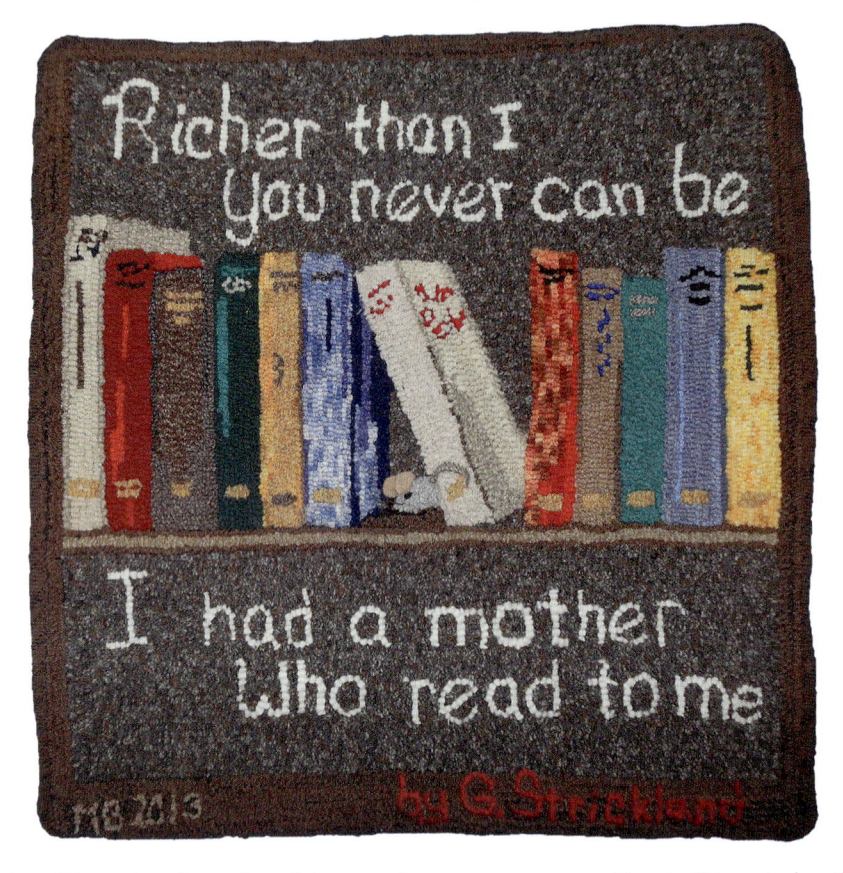

A Mother Who Read to Me, 22" x 18", #3- through 5-cut wool on cotton rug warp, with embellishments described below. Designed and hooked by Marilyn Becker, Wausau, Wisconsin, 2014.

"My daughter, who loves books, has been a librarian for 18 years," Marilyn said. "I believe her love of books came from me, and mine from my mother. Her two daughters are also bookworms. She mentioned this quote, and I thought a rug would be the best way to display it on her library wall. The verse is from Strickland Gillian. His entire poem is as follows: 'You may have tangible wealth untold, caskets of jewels and coffers of gold. Richer than I you can never be. I had a mother who read to me.'

"The little mouse in the center is sculptured (Waldoboro style) with proddy ears and a simple #6-cut piece of wool with a knot at the end. I added a black bead for the eye and some fishing line for the whiskers. My daughter loved it."

Whenever I think about hooking beliefs, Deanne Fitzpatrick comes to mind. From the moment I saw it, I loved her rug that urges the viewer to "Create beauty every day." She lives by that motto, and it hangs on a wall where she and her fellow hookers can absorb those encouraging words. Some of the most popular commercial rug patterns express commonly held beliefs in a word, a phrase, or a pithy sentence like Deanne's.

This design idea invites you to consider putting your beliefs in writing on a rug. If nothing springs to mind, peruse your own bookshelves or look online for the proverbs, quotations, affirmations, or brief personal mission statements that give voice to your beliefs. Greeting cards are surprisingly good sources, as are the quotations on your daily calendar. A line or two from a favorite poem, the lyrics of a memorable song, or a statement from a hero might be the best way of putting our beliefs or philosophies on our walls or floors, where we will see them every day and be inspired. Hooking beliefs is a special kind of meditation that allows us to ruminate on meaning as we pull the loops that form the words.

Some rug designs of this nature are mostly pictures with just a word or two of text placed strategically in the design. Others are mostly wording, with a flower or a flourish to make them pretty. But however we approach hooking meaningful words, we must give some thought to methods of hooking letters of the alphabet.

Love Many, Trust Few, *13³⁄₁₀" x 13³⁄₁₀", #4-cut wool on linen. Designed and hooked by Trish Johnson, Toronto, Ontario, 2003.*

"This is an old autograph verse that my Uncle Cecil wrote in my mother's autograph book," Trish said, "and that my mother wrote in mine. It is a variation on another favorite of hers: 'to thine own self be true.' The image is of my son Douglas, about 17 years old, at Camp Pinecrest in the Muskokas. My children are lucky to have spent most of their summers at camp jumping off rocks into clear water. I wanted the border to be reminiscent of native quillwork. When I went to camp, native crafts were the cat's meow. This could also be titled Mother's Advice. One of the hardest parts of being a mother is letting your children go—to camp, or out in a canoe, or to university. At some point, your children really do have to paddle their own canoes.

"I buy plaid scarves at Goodwill that are the colors of the Canadian landscape, blue skies, green trees (orange and red in the fall), grey rocks, brown tree trunks. Brown doesn't occur on the color wheel, but I think of it as dark orange." Trish crocheted the edge of this rug, rather than whipping it.

Fortunately for me, two of my teachers have shared expertise on hooking letters. In workshops with Pris Buttler and Sharon Townsend, these teachers included booklets or handouts on the techniques they have developed for hooking letters that are legible, attractive, and well suited to the meaning they express. Since I don't hook letters very often, I tend to pull out these useful reference guides whenever I need them.

Perhaps the easiest approach to hooking lettering is to simply write out our words in our own handwriting. Some designs are very well suited to a handwritten look. When something more formal seems appropriate, though, look to your library of fonts.

"Font" is a word that relatively few people used 30 years ago. Today, with word processing functions on every home computer, we can all become familiar with fonts, which are typefaces of various sizes, weights, and styles. Would you like something that looks as though it had been typed on an old typewriter, or do the stylized fonts of the Arts and Crafts movement appeal to you? Determine whether you're going for an old-fashioned look or a modern one, a casual effect or the look of formal engraving. I have found it helpful to make drafts with paper and pencil first, getting the size and spacing of the letters exactly as I want them, before I put marker to linen.

Design Idea #2: Slice-of-Life Story

Art itself is nothing but the attempt to catch one particular moment . . . and make it everlasting.

—Karen Blixon

Admiring the Rug, 38" x 33", recycled fabrics, sheep's fleece, wool yarn, and old blankets on hessian backing. Designed and hooked by Diane Cox, Penzance, Cornwall, 2013.

"This rug really is a slice of life," Diane said, "a frequent occurrence amongst rug hookers. The small, ordinary, domestic parts of life are very important to me, having a chat with friends, sharing a pot of tea, eating homemade cake, getting excited about color, fabrics, and design, being cozy indoors when it's grey and gloomy outside. I make at least one proddy mat each winter. They keep you warm whilst you are prodding. I wanted to mix proddy with hooking in this piece, so in this picture, I like to think I am showing off my latest winter proddy mat to my friend."

We have already explored the idea of hooking the important milestones of our lives into story rugs. This design idea is quite different. Rather than the big moments, here we will ponder those everyday events that make up the fabric of our lives.

Our everyday chores make excellent fodder for this design idea. Raking fall leaves, hanging sheets on the line, watering the ivy in a sunny window: these chores are integral to our days and suggest a well-loved home.

Ruminate on your simple moments among family or friends, popping popcorn together, enjoying the newspaper and morning coffee, or playing with a dear pet. Many a rug hooker has hooked a rug that shows women hooking together.

Diane Cox's *Admiring the Rug* is an example. She has depicted that pleasurable moment when one woman shows her friend the finished item, all hooked and bound. While we might be able to hook a simple room or scene, chances are that this slice-of-life design idea will require hooking the human form, something that can seem intimidating when we haven't done it before. Remember two things, please:

Embrace What You Can Do

Let's look at the rugs of someone who is arguably the most well-known rug hooker in North America, Deanne Fitzpatrick. The human beings featured in many of her slice-of-life rugs are without facial detail. She simply doesn't hook their features; rather, she suggests facial expression through subtle touches of shading. She invests a great deal of imagination in their dresses, hats, purses, and shoes. These clothing items begin to imply personality. The posture of the figure, the demeanor, the tilt of the head—all of these help the viewer to mentally infer the face and its expression. So please don't allow self-doubt to interfere with your slice-of-life rug. Draw and hook. And remember, WWW (wool works wonders).

Use the Tools Available to You

Go back to Chapter 2 and get busy investigating the resources available, such as "how to draw" tutorials abound on YouTube. You will find books and DVDs that can teach you how to hook the human form. No excuses. Imagine what you want to draw, and then be self-directed in learning how to do it.

Folk Life Rug of Pris Buttler, *40" x 55", #4-, 6- and 8-cut wool on linen. Designed and hooked by Pris Buttler, Gainesville, Georgia, 2002.*
  Our slice-of-life example from Pris Buttler is really many slices of life, all in a single rug. The tiny vignettes include the various landscapes and people important to her life story.
  "This rug was done when the Azari folk life rugs were popular," Pris said. Texas-born, she incorporated imagery from the Lone Star State: "Folklore of Navajo woven rugs says that one thread exits the rug on each side; therefore, the rug's spirit can enter and exit. So my steers in the border are leaving the picture plane." She included her parents in Aruba and her adolescent years in Venezuela. Generation after generation, pets and family members populate the scenes. Her wedding in New Mexico, the astrological sign she shares with her husband (they were born on the same day), the paint palette of Pris's profession, and scenes that include her children and grandchildren: all are part of this folk life rug.

Start with You **131**

Design Idea #3: Hook a Better World

Sometimes I have a cause that haunts me until I grab it, and pin it down, and make a rug that illustrates it. Illustrating it makes it real. Making it real raises awareness.

—Donna Hrkman

Through My Eyes, *12" x 16", #3-through 5-cut wool on linen. Adapted from a photograph by Edward S. Curtis. Designed and hooked by Lou Ann Ayres, Papillion, Nebraska, 2014.*

"I adapted Curtis's photograph," Lou Ann said," taken to document the Native American people before their populations dwindled. His work was donated to the Library of Congress and made available to all to help keep their spirit alive. One can almost see the wisdom behind the eyes. I am sure we all agree that rug hooking is an art form. Art is a means of expressing yourself and honoring others. Doing a partially finished piece while showing some elements of design on canvas hopefully will help others see this as an art form and seek to understand. The unfinished canvas also helps the image come off the canvas and tell us their story."

Donna Hrkman calls them "awareness rugs." They are hooked for a cause important to the hooker. Donna's book, *Creative Techniques for Rug Hookers*, shows us several of her cause rugs, honoring our veterans, speaking out against abuse, and giving a voice to victims who have no voice. All of us have such causes that we care about. The beautiful swirl of a hooked pink ribbon, for instance, holds worlds of meaning to my hooking group, among whom many have come through a diagnosis and treatment.

When we volunteer our time or make monetary donations, we support the things that are important to us, to our families, or to our communities. This design idea asks you to give some thought to hooking those values and passions into a rug. If you give to the Humane Society, you may be inspired to hook a rug that encourages the ethical treatment of animals. If you fear for endangered species, create a design that brings awareness to that cause. If a loved one or acquaintance is fighting a battle—a physical health issue, a mental health issue, or even a civil rights issue—your rug can show support. We can give these rugs as gifts of empathy or display them to lend our support.

The two rugs featured here make interesting examples of cause rugs. Laura Kenney of Truro, Nova Scotia, learned that many of the historic Nova Scotia lighthouses are in danger, as they were declared surplus by the Federal Government. She felt that her province was losing part of its history, "part of ourselves," she said. "And so, I began a series of lighthouse rugs to tell this story."

Lou Ann Ayres's rug is an adaptation of a photograph by Edward S. Curtis, 1868–1952. Curtis's photographs capture a disappearing culture, as described by a website that chronicles his life: "Having become deeply impassioned by the power and dignity of the American Indian, Curtis began to realize for the first time that he might create a record preserving the history of these magnificent people and their extraordinary culture."

What causes speak to you? Do some research, if necessary. Look into the organizations that support causes about which you are passionate. Then, use your sketchbook to hone the design of your first awareness rug.

Call for Help, *11½" x 31", #8-cut wool, yarn, sari ribbon, and burlap on linen. Designed and hooked by Laura Kenney, Truro, Nova Scotia, 2014.*

After learning that many historic lighthouses in Nova Scotia were to be closed, Laura took action to make the public aware that a piece of the province's history was in danger of being lost. "I learned through reading Chris Mills's book, Lighthouse Legacies, *that before the days of wireless communication, if there was trouble on the island, the only way the lighthouse keeper could get the attention of the mainland was to hang a red cloth from the clothesline. So from this image, came the idea for* Call for Help.

Design Idea #4: Heritage and Genealogy

*My husband is a descendant of William the Conqueror—
not that I intend to start treating him like royalty.*

—Janet Conner

For many of us, the understanding of where we come from is vague at best. "Irish on my mother's side, German on my dad's." That's what I used to recite when someone asked my ancestry. What happened before my grandparents' generation was unclear. But someone in our family found our paternal great-grandfather's papers from when he came through Ellis Island at age 17, and suddenly other pieces of the puzzle started coming together. The little book of good wishes from his parents and all of his friends was found, and we had it translated from German into English. We located and acquired the small wooden trunk that carried everything he owned across the ocean, with the words "Davenport, Iowa, North Amerika" still faintly visible on the top. Great-Grandpa Petersen had always been the bearded man in the sepia photograph. But he became someone else in our imaginations. He was once a teenager who left everyone he loved to make his way in a new place.

To examine and commemorate our heritage asks us to look back, sometimes way, way back, into other worlds. Sometimes a search for images is done mentally, by constructing the past from knowledge, story, and imagination. Other times the images we seek can be found in family albums, libraries, in genealogical artifacts, or even on the Internet. The important thing is to do the seeking.

If it's still possible to talk with the elders of your family, take that opportunity. Documents can tell us a great deal, but there's nothing like a firsthand story for bringing the past to life.

Our heritage might be depicted in symbols, like a family crest or shield. A scene or a place, such as a German milking barn or the green fields of Ireland, could also convey the home and the life of an ancestor.

Marilyn Becker has invested a great deal of time researching her family history, and she was fortunate to find paintings of ancestors from the sixteenth century! One of those, which Marilyn adapted, is shown here. Janet Conner's husband can trace his lineage to William the Conqueror. These are extraordinary examples of successful research. Regardless of how far you have taken your genealogical exploration, consider preserving some aspect of it in a hooked rug. The finished piece will be cherished by your family and will give future generations a key to their own heritage.

134 Designed By You

OPPOSITE PAGE: King William's Ship, *50" x 36", hand-cut wool (variable in width, but equal to a #5- through 7-cut) on linen. Adapted from the embroidery of the Bayeaux Tapestry. Designed and hooked by Janet Conner, Hiram, Maine, 2014.*

Janet used all hand-dyed and heirloom wools in this project. "My husband's family can trace their genealogy to William the Conqueror, so I thought he might like this rug, an adaptation of one small part of the famous Bayeaux Tapestry, made over the period of 1066 to 1070. Today, the tapestry is housed in a museum in Normandy. It is actually not a tapestry at all. It is a masterwork of hand embroidery, over 640 feet in length and about 24 inches high. It tells the story of William the Conqueror's Norman invasion of England in the year 1066." About the unevenness, Janet said, "it was intentional, as this is how the original fabric looks after almost 945 years!"

14 Great-Grand Aunt Agnes, *16" x 20", #3- and 4-cut wool on cotton rug warp. Designed and hooked by Marilyn Becker, Wausau, Wisconsin, 2014.*

"I am a member of Ancestry.com," Marilyn said, "and am always gathering more documented items related to my lineage. Imagine my surprise when I found a photo of a painting of my aunt and also one of her tombstone in Germany. I also found photos of paintings of her father, husband, and daughter. They took my breath away. I just had to do a rug of her beautiful face. She was born in 1490 and died in 1530 at age 40. She had 13 children in 13 years and died in childbirth. She was married to the president of the University of Tubingen, Germany where he was the professor of law. This rug was a pleasure to hook."

Start with You **135**

Design Idea #5: Play It Again, Sam: Hooking a Series

Repetition is the mother of learning, the father of action, which makes it the architect of accomplishment.

—Zig Ziglar

Hanging Out the Lighthouse, *13" x 28", #8-cut wool, yarn, and sari-silk ribbon on burlap. Designed and hooked by Laura Kenney, Truro, Nova Scotia, 2014*

Hanging Out the Cats, *11½" x 31", #8-cut wool, yarn, and sari-silk ribbon on burlap. Designed and hooked by Laura Kenney, Truro,*

136 Designed By You

Hanging Him Out to Dry, *13" x 31", #8-cut wool, yarn, and sari-silk ribbon on burlap. Designed and hooked by Laura Kenney, Truro, Nova Scotia, 2011.*

"When I hook a series," Laura said, "it isn't intentional. I guess it is, but it's just that my mind keeps going back to the subject. With the clothesline series, initially I just wanted to put something other than clothes on the line, as I thought it would be interesting. So it started with fish on the line. Then a husband! Cats, lighthouses, and so on. It's fun to go back to it again and again, as it feels familiar and I know I will be happy with how it turns out. It's like comfort food."

Ice skaters do their figure-eights. Piano students play their scales. Any art requires practice and repetition. Certainly, we practice every time we pick up our hooks.

But we can take our practice a little deeper by finding an image we love and hooking variations of it. Vincent Van Gogh's sunflowers, Monet's lilies, Georgia O'Keeffe's opening blossoms—it's an artistic tradition to deepen understanding by doing multiple versions of a particular subject.

In a series, you don't need to hook enormous rugs. I have seen several series of tiny pieces. Perhaps hooking a small spring landscape will lead you to hook the same scene in summer, autumn, and winter. Perhaps by hooking a red door, you'll take an interest in hooking many different kinds of doors. One of my hooking role models, Deanne Fitzpatrick, has hooked many, many series, finding more and more variations on the current theme, until her imagination moves on to the next one.

After I had been hooking for a while, I realized that I'd done quite a few crows. For whatever reason, these unruly black birds excite my imagination, and I continue to hook one now and then. For you, it could be that an artist takes your fancy, prompting you to hook several adaptations—of Cezanne or Gauguin or Klee. Debra Smith has hooked a series of what she calls "sisters rugs." She has four sisters, and she has found opportunities—in various styles—to hook five women into a rug.

Laura Kenney and Roslyn Logsdon are both accomplished hookers of series. Space will allow us to show you only a few rugs from Laura's entertaining clothesline series and from Roslyn's exalting gothic arches.

Start with You 137

Washington Cathedral, *21" x 29½", #3-cut wool on linen. Designed and hooked by Roslyn Logsdon, Laurel, Maryland, 2008.*

"Gothic arches intrigue me," Roslyn Logsdon said. "Their lines reach for the sky." They intrigue her so much, in fact, that Roslyn has hooked no fewer than 17 Gothic-arch rugs to date. In Washington Cathedral, she started with the off-kilter perspective of a viewer gazing up at arches within arches. "I created the illusion of depth by the use of color," she said. "There are no green walls at the Washington Cathedral, but that fabric just wanted to be used. The shapes were simplified to stress the upward movement."

Santa Maria del Mar (Barcelona), *24" x 27", #3-cut wool on linen. Designed and hooked by Roslyn Logsdon, Laurel, Maryland, 2007.*

"I have been lucky enough to visit many cathedrals and monasteries in Great Britain and Europe," Roslyn said. "Each one is different, showing variations on a theme. Many were built eight to nine thousand years ago. The fact that they are still standing is amazing. Santa Maria del Mar, in Barcelona, is an example of fourteenth century Catalan Gothic architecture. What spoke to me on entering was the different light and space."

Brown Gothic, *25" x 16½", #3-cut wool on linen. Designed and hooked by Roslyn Logsdon, Laurel, Maryland, 2015.*

"As I saw more Gothic architecture," Roslyn said, "one of my aims was to create the space between the arches as they soared up to the vaulting. I wanted the space to recede into the darkness. As I did more variations, the exact location of the cathedral disappeared and what remained was the construction, space, and uniqueness of each one."

Start with You **139**

Design Idea #6: My Mirror

Everything we make, however lofty or low, reveals and resonates with ourselves. We might as well be purposeful with it.

—Wanda Kerr

We have reached the final design idea in this final chapter on expressing ourselves through our hooking. After discussing many ways of doing that, we arrive at perhaps the most direct means of self-expression—creating a self-portrait. Rug hooking can be a mirror in which we laugh with and at ourselves, imagine other selves we could become, reflect things we cherish, or observe the new versions of ourselves that appear with the passing of each decade, each year, even each day.

There are as many ways to hook a self-portrait as there are rug hookers, and we'd like to show you several creative examples, beginning with the *Alter Ego* of Diane Cox. I used to think an alter ego was the opposite of oneself, but really, it's just another kind of self, someone we might have been, someone we could become, someone who has just awakened inside us.

Håkon Grøn Hensvold of Norway creates enormous rugs filled with meaningful imagery and personal symbolism. His self-portrait is no exception, including significant names and dates, his home, and his children, as well as certain symbols that he would like to remain a mystery, open to the interpretation of the viewer. One aspect of the portrait that he does discuss is his dazzling beard, hooked in many colors. Although it is turning gray in real life, he hooked it to reflect the colors he carries inside him.

Wanda Kerr has hooked many realistic self-portraits, and this one astonishes with its beauty, as well as with the surprisingly wide-cut wool used to make it. While hooking a rug of herself hooking a rug, Wanda used a #12-cut and wider.

Known for her sense of humor, Kay LeFevre created this fanciful self-portrait, *Wool Genie*. Kay hooks with yarn, and she incorporated other textiles and fibers into the piece. Her example shows us that a self-portrait needn't be so serious, but can give us a chance to laugh.

In addition to Norma Brimstein's own image, she hooked her sentiment about the importance of art in her life.

To continue the echo of Chapter 2 on ways of drawing, if you can type a few search terms, you can educate yourself on drawing your own face. Search "tutorial on drawing self-portrait," and revel in the results. Put your digital camera in someone else's hands and strike a pose! Choose a favorite photo; crop or distort at will. Online, you can check out Wanda Kerr's online classroom, The Welcome Mat. Purchase books on hooking portraits from wonderful authors Anne Marie Littenberg and April DeConick. And then create your first mirror-rug in wool.

OPPOSITE PAGE: Puss Crosby, Alter Ego, *26" x 52", recycled fabrics, knitting yarns, hand-spun wool, sari silk, and a knitted woolen sweater on hessian. Designed and hooked by Diane Cox, Penzance, Cornwall, 2012.*

After reading Wanda Kerr's amusing way of working out your hooking alter ego name—the name of your very first pet and the name of the first road you lived on—I thought it would be fun for our hooking group to work out our hooking alter egos and hook them.

My alter-ego name was Puss Crosby, and I pondered on this name for a long time, especially during my dog walks. Gradually she began to emerge inside my head. I started to make sketches and eventually drew her out quite simply on the hessian. Whilst hooking, I was listening to music and a phrase in Crosby, Stills & Nash's "Suite, Judy Blue Eyes" seemed to resonate with me: "How can you catch the s parrow?" So that question was hooked into her. I deliberately wanted the words to appear a bit fuzzy, because Puss was thinking them, not speaking them. The wings came about halfway through, not planned at all.

Altogether it was a magical experience hooking her. I just let it flow with few expectations. At the end, I realized that she had become very meaningful to me. The sturdy boots symbolize being grounded. The flowers growing up the boots represent a love of nature. The apron means domesticity, and the cat means female intuition. The tiny insignificant bird is a wise old soul, and her wings are freedom and the means of escaping whenever she feels like it."

RIGHT: Self Portrait, *45" x 67", #5-cut wool on linen. Designed and hooked by Håkon Grøn Hensvold, Skreia, Norway, 2011.*

"Creating a self-portrait is a challenge," Håkon said, "because it reflects yourself. Those who look at it when it's finished should see who you are and what you stand for. It is difficult.

"I wanted to put things that are important to me into my design. My children and our house are in the center of my beard. My wife's name, Lilian, is in the heart at the left. I collect 'hoya,' a houseplant. I have about 150 different hoya, so I had to put in one such flower. The border is my memo pad for old dates: my birthday, my wedding, my children's birthdays, and the names of my mother and father and my siblings.

"The rest of the symbols are a little harder to tell you about. It is my own symbolic language that I create and that you will find in my other work. A house. The flower. The eye and others. I want these symbols to be open to interpretation and leave the viewer to make their own opinion. Why do I have a colored beard? It's about to be gray in real life. I think it's my way to show the colors that are inside me."

Start with You 141

(My Mirror continued)

Town Hooker, 30" x 42", #12- to 16-cut wool and nylon on linen. Designed and hooked by Wanda Kerr, Wiarton, Ontario, 2003.

When designing this self-portrait, Wanda wanted "something that felt like it represented the true me. It had to be big. I liked the joke of me hooking a rug of me hooking a rug. I also loved the perversity of hooking a portrait in a #12 cut. I like to break stereotypes.

"This was the first self-portrait I hooked, and I've done several since that time. I enjoy portraying myself through my own filter, not as a mother, wife, teacher, granny, or friend, but just what I'm seeing and feeling at any given point in time. I enjoy watching myself age and change and adapt to each stage in my life in my self-portrait hookings.

"No matter what we create, we are telling strikingly true stories of ourselves," Wanda said, "whether we mean to or not. What we create is an extension of our nature, and everything we make reveals and resonates of ourselves, however lofty or low. We might as well be purposeful in it."

Self Portrait with Pen, 16" x 19", #5- and 8-cut wool on linen. Designed and hooked by Norma Brimstein, Rochester, New York.

"Nothing defines me better than my desire to solve a puzzle of any kind," Norma said. "So I put myself in a crossword background. It's also an honest recognition of what I spend way too much time doing. In an attempt to appear somewhat more profound, I included one of my favorite quotes. It had to be edited a tad to fit it into the grid. Those are all complete words behind me, even though you can't see them in their entirety, which speaks to my perfectionist nature. The title is Self Portrait with Pen, *because I never use a pencil.*

Wool Genie, 24" x 30", yarn on rug warp. Designed and hooked by Kay LeFevre, Windsor, Ontario, 2012.

"This is a fantasy self-portrait," Kay said, "done for a rug challenge. Rub the lamp and maybe you'll get some magic wool! She is hooked with yarn, and the top and harem pants are from a scarf and bra bought at Goodwill for pennies. The shoes are gold glitter material I had kicking around the house. The fantasy part comes from being able to show off my tummy and have a sexy belly button. Those were the days, eh? I use this design for my Facebook profile photo."

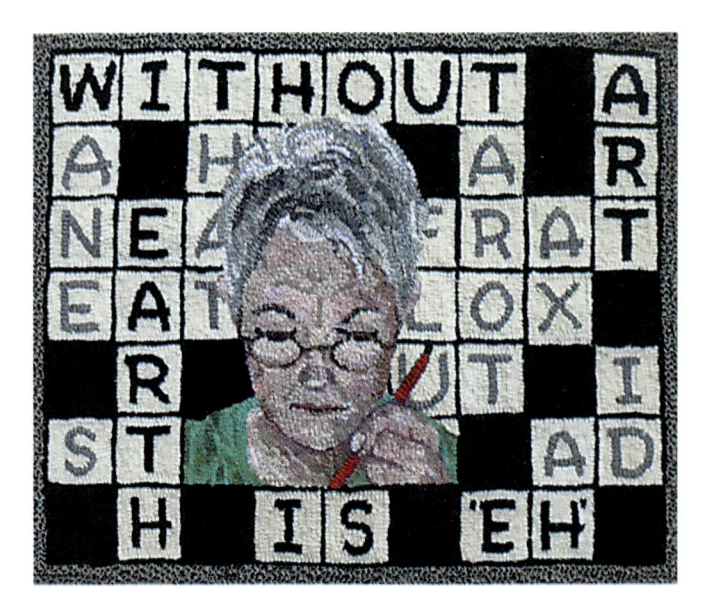

Recommendations for Further Inspiration

ABOUT BECOMING AN ARTIST

Bayles, David, and Ted Orland. *Art and Fear: Observations on the Perils and Rewards of Artmaking*. Image Continuing Press, 2001.

Buttler, Pris. *Basic Design & Drawing Techniques for the Rug Hooker*. 2000. Order this useful booklet by emailing prisrugs@charter.net.

Cardaci, Diane, et al. *Drawing Concepts*. Walter Foster Publishing, 2009.

Kleon, Austin. *Steal Like an Artist: 10 Things Nobody Told You About Being Creative*. Workman Publishing Company, 2012.

Roberts, Ian. *Mastering Composition*. Northlight Books, 2008. DVD included.

ABOUT COLOR

Pavich, Tamara. Straying Off the Color Wheel: Achromatic Rug Hooking. *Rug Hooking* magazine, September/October 2015.

———. The Blue Period: Expanding Creativity through Monochromatic Rugs. *Rug Hooking* magazine, November/December, 2014.

Wolfrom, Joen. *Color Play*. C&T Publishing, 2000. Color by color, the author explores various schemes. This excellent quilting book is easily relatable to rug hooking.

———. *The Ultimate 3-in-1 Color Tool*. C&T Publishing, 2011. This tool contains 24 color cards with numbered swatches, 5 color ins for each color, and 2 value finders, red green. This quilting tool helps a reader stand color schemes—complements, and monochromatics.

ART AND ART
ON

and Jacqueline M. Atkins.
ican Life. Viking Studio

Doodle Rugs: Doodle Your
. *Rug Hooking* magazine,
st 2013.

Fitzpatrick, Deanne. *Beginning to Hook Abstract Rugs*. Deanne Fitzpatrick's self-paced online course gives students access to video lessons, photos, and written explanations of the concept and the process. Find out more at http://www.hookingrugs.com/.

———. *Simply Modern: Contemporary Designs for Hooked Rugs*. Nimbus Publishing, 2014.

Pavich, Tamara. Learning from the Masters: Fine Art Inspiration for Rug Hookers. *Rug Hooking* magazine, September/November, 2014

———. Love Stories: Asking Permission to Adapt Contemporary Art. *Rug Hooking* magazine, March/April/May 2015.

———. Post-Impressionist Rug Hooking. *Rug Hooking* magazine, June/July/August 2015.

———. Van Gogh Vibrations. *Rug Hooking* magazine, March/April/May 2016.

———. Variations on Klimt. *Rug Hooking* magazine, November/December 2011.

ABOUT TEXTILE ARTS AND FIBERS

Lewis, Alfred Allan. *The Mountain Artisans Quilting Book*. Macmillan, 1973. Used copies readily available for a great price.

Newman, Thelma R. *Quilting, Patchwork, Applique, and Trapunto: Traditional Methods and Original Designs*. Crown Publishing, 1974. Available from online sellers of used books.

Pavich, Tamara. New Spins on Fabric: A Gallery of Textile-Inspired Rugs. *Rug Hooking* magazine, November/December 2015.

Schoeser, Mary. *Textiles: The Art of Mankind*. Thames and Hudson, 2012. Comprehensive treatment of worldwide textiles; a hefty volume with a hefty price tag.

Taylor, Judy. *Joy of Hooking with Yarn*. Little House Rugs, 2011.

———. *Rug Hooker's Guide to the Yarnverse!* Little House Rugs, 2011.

ABOUT STORY RUG DESIGNS

Fitzpatrick, Deanne. *Hook Me a Story: The History and Method of Rug Hooking in Atlantic Canada*. Nimbus Publishing, 1999.

———. *Inspired Rug-Hooking: Turning Atlantic Canadian Life into Art*. Nimbus Publishing, 2010.

Hackman, Paulette. *Story Rugs and their Storytellers: Rug Hooking in the Narrative Style*. *Rug Hooking* magazine, 2016.

Pavich, Tamara. Forty Shades of Brown: A Lesson in Hooking Sepia Rugs. *Rug Hooking* magazine, March/April/May 2014

VERY HELPFUL RUG-HOOKING BOOKS AND PUBLICATIONS

Buttler, Pris. *Easy Lettering Tips for the Rug Hooker*. 2000. Order this useful booklet by emailing prisrugs@charter.net.

DeConick, April D. *Wool Snapshots: A Rug Hooker's Guide to Creating Miniature Portraits from Photos*. Red Jack Rugs, 2013.

Dufresne, Gail. *Geometric Hooked Rugs: Color and Design*. *Rug Hooking* magazine, 2010.

Eaton, Doris. *A Lifetime of Rug-Hooking*. Nimbus Publishing, 2011.

Hrkman, Donna. *Creative Techniques for Rug-Hookers*. *Rug Hooking* magazine, 2015.

Littenberg, Anne-Marie. *Hooked Rug Portraits*. *Rug Hooking* magazine, 2011.

Norwood, Cynthia Smesny. *Creating an Antique Look in Hand-Hooked Rugs*. *Rug Hooking* magazine, 2008.

———. *Primitive Hooked Rugs for the 21st Century*. *Rug Hooking* magazine, 2015.

Rex, Stella Hay. *Practical Hooked Rugs: How to Design and Make Them at Home*. Prentice-Hall, 1949. Available online from used booksellers.

Shepherd, Gene, with Jane Olson. *The Rug Hooker's Bible*. *Rug Hooking* magazine, 2005.

Recommendations for Further Inspiration

ABOUT BECOMING AN ARTIST

Bayles, David, and Ted Orland. *Art and Fear: Observations on the Perils and Rewards of Artmaking*. Image Continuing Press, 2001.

Buttler, Pris. *Basic Design & Drawing Techniques for the Rug Hooker*. 2000. Order this useful booklet by emailing prisrugs@charter.net.

Cardaci, Diane, et al. *Drawing Concepts*. Walter Foster Publishing, 2009.

Kleon, Austin. *Steal Like an Artist: 10 Things Nobody Told You About Being Creative*. Workman Publishing Company, 2012.

Roberts, Ian. *Mastering Composition*. Northlight Books, 2008. DVD included.

ABOUT COLOR

Pavich, Tamara. Straying Off the Color Wheel: Achromatic Rug Hooking. *Rug Hooking* magazine, September/October 2015.

———. The Blue Period: Expanding Creativity through Monochromatic Rugs. *Rug Hooking* magazine, November/December, 2014.

Wolfrom, Joen. *Color Play*. C&T Publishing, 2000. Color by color, the author explores various schemes. This excellent quilting book is easily relatable to rug hooking.

———. *The Ultimate 3-in-1 Color Tool*. C&T Publishing, 2011. This tool contains 24 color cards with numbered swatches, 5 color plans for each color, and 2 value finders, red and green. This quilting tool helps a reader understand color schemes—complements, triads, and monochromatics.

ABOUT ART AND ART ADAPTATION

Bishop, Robert, and Jacqueline M. Atkins. *Folk Art in American Life*. Viking Studio Books, 1995.

Cameron, Cilla. Doodle Rugs: Doodle Your Way to a Design. *Rug Hooking* magazine, June/July/August 2013.

Fitzpatrick, Deanne. *Beginning to Hook Abstract Rugs*. Deanne Fitzpatrick's self-paced online course gives students access to video lessons, photos, and written explanations of the concept and the process. Find out more at http://www.hookingrugs.com/.

———. *Simply Modern: Contemporary Designs for Hooked Rugs*. Nimbus Publishing, 2014.

Pavich, Tamara. Learning from the Masters: Fine Art Inspiration for Rug Hookers. *Rug Hooking* magazine, September/November, 2014

———. Love Stories: Asking Permission to Adapt Contemporary Art. *Rug Hooking* magazine, March/April/May 2015.

———. Post-Impressionist Rug Hooking. *Rug Hooking* magazine, June/July/August 2015.

———. Van Gogh Vibrations. *Rug Hooking* magazine, March/April/May 2016.

———. Variations on Klimt. *Rug Hooking* magazine, November/December 2011.

ABOUT TEXTILE ARTS AND FIBERS

Lewis, Alfred Allan. *The Mountain Artisans Quilting Book*. Macmillan, 1973. Used copies readily available for a great price.

Newman, Thelma R. *Quilting, Patchwork, Applique, and Trapunto: Traditional Methods and Original Designs*. Crown Publishing, 1974. Available from online sellers of used books.

Pavich, Tamara. New Spins on Fabric: A Gallery of Textile-Inspired Rugs. *Rug Hooking* magazine, November/December 2015.

Schoeser, Mary. *Textiles: The Art of Mankind*. Thames and Hudson, 2012. Comprehensive treatment of worldwide textiles; a hefty volume with a hefty price tag.

Taylor, Judy. *Joy of Hooking with Yarn*. Little House Rugs, 2011.

———. *Rug Hooker's Guide to the Yarniverse!* Little House Rugs, 2011.

ABOUT STORY RUG DESIGNS

Fitzpatrick, Deanne. *Hook Me a Story: The History and Method of Rug Hooking in Atlantic Canada*. Nimbus Publishing, 1999.

———. *Inspired Rug-Hooking: Turning Atlantic Canadian Life into Art*. Nimbus Publishing, 2010.

Hackman, Paulette. *Story Rugs and their Storytellers: Rug Hooking in the Narrative Style*. *Rug Hooking* magazine, 2016.

Pavich, Tamara. Forty Shades of Brown: A Lesson in Hooking Sepia Rugs. *Rug Hooking* magazine, March/April/May 2014

VERY HELPFUL RUG-HOOKING BOOKS AND PUBLICATIONS

Buttler, Pris. *Easy Lettering Tips for the Rug Hooker*. 2000. Order this useful booklet by emailing prisrugs@charter.net.

DeConick, April D. *Wool Snapshots: A Rug Hooker's Guide to Creating Miniature Portraits from Photos*. Red Jack Rugs, 2013.

Dufresne, Gail. *Geometric Hooked Rugs: Color and Design*. *Rug Hooking* magazine, 2010.

Eaton, Doris. *A Lifetime of Rug-Hooking*. Nimbus Publishing, 2011.

Hrkman, Donna. *Creative Techniques for Rug-Hookers*. *Rug Hooking* magazine, 2015.

Littenberg, Anne-Marie. *Hooked Rug Portraits*. *Rug Hooking* magazine, 2011.

Norwood, Cynthia Smesny. *Creating an Antique Look in Hand-Hooked Rugs*. *Rug Hooking* magazine, 2008.

———. *Primitive Hooked Rugs for the 21st Century*. *Rug Hooking* magazine, 2015.

Rex, Stella Hay. *Practical Hooked Rugs: How to Design and Make Them at Home*. Prentice-Hall, 1949. Available online from used booksellers.

Shepherd, Gene, with Jane Olson. *The Rug Hooker's Bible*. *Rug Hooking* magazine, 2005.

In Conclusion

Once I have glanced through a new rug hooking book, I usually keep it at my bedside for a closer read, or in my hooking room so I can look back at topics or photos or share favorite parts with my hooking friends. Whether you've designed dozens of your own rugs or are just beginning to design, here are some ways that you can use this book . . .

Troll for Inspiration
The next time you browse through these pages, go slowly, paying attention to your own responses and personal connections that may arise from design ideas and rug photos. Mark favorite pages with reminders on sticky notes ("Go through Andy's baby pictures."), jot down suggestions ("Sketch a dark-light log cabin design."), or make a note of encouragement ("It's high time to try out embellishments!"). When you're ready to start a new rug, those colorful notes will be like bread crumbs, leading you to your next design.

Choose a Self-Assignment
To go a little deeper, look at those design ideas you marked with sticky notes and list them on a sheet of paper. Write a little bit about each and why it appeals to you, and then make a prioritized list. Are most of your sticky notes in one chapter? Then maybe you're heading into an art phase, a new color palette, or a spate of story rugs. Your ultimate goal is to give yourself one new assignment—a personal challenge.

Try a Group Challenge
Self-assignments can be contagious. As you share your new designs with hooking friends, they may want in on the action. Any of these thirty-six design ideas can become a group challenge, with lots of room for unique variations on a common theme.

Having come to the end of this writing project, I feel the urge to go straight to my sketchbook and draw. There's so much here that I haven't yet tried, and these examples provide just the nudge I needed. Textiles, particularly African mud cloth and vintage quilts, are calling to me. I have more family photos to hook. And I feel a fit of whimsy coming on, a need for more colorful characters in my hooking room.

If you would like to read more deeply about designing around style, color, art, materials, story, or your own identity, check out the suggested reading list.

Thank you for reading. I wish you courage, patience, and delight as you design and hook expressions of yourself.